THE RELATE GUIDE TO LOVING IN LATER LIFE

Intimacy in the prime of life

Marj Thoburn and
Suzy Powling

VERMILION
London

First published in Great Britain in 2000

Text © Suzy Powling, Marj Thoburn and Relate 2000

Suzy Powling has asserted her rights to be identified as the Author of this work under the Copyright, Designs and Patents Act 1988

First published in 2000 by Vermilion an imprint of Ebury Press
Random House, 20 Vauxhall Bridge Road, London SW1V 2SA

The Random House Group Limited supports The Forest Stewardship Council® (FSC®), the leading international forest-certification organisation. Our books carrying the FSC label are printed on FSC®-certified paper. FSC is the only forest-certification scheme supported by the leading environmental organisations, including Greenpeace. Our paper procurement policy can be found at www.randomhouse.co.uk/environment

Random House UK Limited Reg. No. 954009

www.randomhouse.co.uk

A CIP catalogue record for this book is available from the British Library.

ISBN 9780091954659

Printed and bound in Great Britain by Clays Ltd, St Ives plc

CONTENTS

ACKNOWLEDGEMENTS

The authors would like to acknowledge the invaluable contributions made to this book by Relate practitioners Pat Bailey, Fran Bradley, Melissa Brooks, Kevin Chandler, Julia Cole, Hazel Jones and Joyce Keith. Ann Logan compiled the list of useful organizations at the end of the book.

Sarah Bowler, Chief Executive of Relate, gave encouragement and support during the writing of this book. Warm thanks are due to colleagues and friends in Relate who have shared their experiences over the years and most importantly to all of those people who have consulted Relate, who have shared their stories and enriched our lives.

'Warning' by Jenny Joseph is taken from *Selected Poems* published by Bloodaxe Books Ltd. Copyright © Jenny Joseph 1992

Table on page 41 'Sources of Conflict and Pleasure' Copyright 1993 © the American Psychological Association. Adapted with permission.

All the case histories in this book are based on those of real people. Names and details have been changed so that the individuals and couples cannot be identified.

Finally, this book has been written primarily with a heterosexual focus but with a recognition that there are universal truths to the human sexual condition, whatever the orientation.

MT & SP

INTRODUCTION

"Young we loved each other, and were ignorant."

W.B. Yeats

All our ideas about men and women, husbands and wives, parents and children are built up in a process so gradual and unconscious that it affects us in ways over which we have little knowledge or control. In our most significant relationships, those ideas show themselves in what we say and do, every day, year after year.

Time was – for our parents, perhaps; certainly for our grandparents and their forebears – when many, if not most, of those ideas were shared by all our social peers, with the result that everybody knew what to expect of life and what was expected of them. But in the twentieth century there have been massive social changes, so far-reaching that it is sometimes difficult to separate cause and effect: two world wars, the rise of an affluent middle class, education for all, women in the labour force, contraception you can rely on, space exploration, computers, mobile phones. . .

Those of us who have reached or passed our fiftieth birthdays have witnessed more changes in our half-century-plus than any previous generation. That is a fact. It would be extraordinary if those changes had not had an effect on what we expect from our personal relationships. It should not come as any surprise that the speed at which society has been moving leaves us feeling a little jet-lagged at times and – so far as

playing our part in a couple relationship is concerned –
bothered and a little bewildered as well.

If you were born in the second quarter of the twentieth
century, the millennium might see you celebrating an
important wedding anniversary or embarking on a new
relationship after the ending of your first; you might be
widowed or divorced. That diversity is part of the modern
social picture. What unites us all – and there are a lot of us –
are the opportunities on offer. We are lucky to have been born
at a time when huge advances in health care would mean that
most of us can look forward to years of active retirement; when
the education we've enjoyed has equipped us to inform and
entertain ourselves; when it's easy, and not too expensive, to
holiday in the sun or visit friends in faraway places. No longer
bound by the nine-to-five routine or the needs of a young
family, we have time and freedom like never before. Life is not
a rehearsal – read on.

_____Chapter One_____

THE WAY WE ARE

Whatever else you may think is lacking at the age of fifty plus, it is not information. Statistics abound, and one of the things they tell us is that the population is getting older, because people are living longer. By the year 2031, it is estimated that 41 per cent of the population will be over fifty, 23 per cent will be over retirement age and 6 per cent will be over eighty. But it is now that society at large is being forced to change its attitude to its older members. This is not just because older people are more vocal than they have been before, nor only that we have all had our sensitivities alerted to underprivileged minorities in general. It is because, as a leader in *The Times* put it in January 1999, 'a growing movement recognises the foolishness of the shallow worship of youth. Older people are increasingly being brought back to the workplace, the television screen and the voluntary organisation. Their experience enriches us'.

Amen to that. But what is it like actually to be one of those older people? What is it like to have reached and to have passed the mid-point of life, to have achieved some of your hopes but surrendered others, to find yourself in the uncharted territory of what we are learning to call 'the third age'? And, most importantly, how is all of this affecting your relationship with your partner? There is little doubt that at this transitional point in life, relationships can suffer: we know that – to reach for the statistics again – 30 per cent of marriages split up when the partners are between forty and sixty. And 'twas not ever thus.

People who married in the early part of the twentieth century were inclined to stay married. There are a number of reasons why, at the end of the century, things have changed. First, people who are discontented with their relationships no longer feel that to be divorced carries a social stigma. Second, women are recognised as men's equals; they are better educated and a force to be reckoned with in the workplace: they can lead independent lives if they want to. But perhaps the greatest change has been in the expectations that men and women have of their intimate relationships with one another: high expectations which take a lot of work if they are to be fulfilled.

Carl Jung, the great nineteenth-century psychoanalyst and student of mankind, said that 'the greatest potential for growth and self-realisation exists in the second half of life'. This is the point at which you might be reviewing your expectations of life and relationships after a long period of just living it, and feeling a little shaken at what you find.

This was how it happened with Kay, who was fifty-five when she left her husband, David. They had met when they were at university together, both serving behind the students' union bar on Friday nights. David graduated in engineering; Kay gained a degree in psychology. They married almost immediately after getting their degrees. David got a good job in an international engineering company and they moved abroad. Kay had become pregnant on honeymoon and having a baby in the first year of marriage meant that she could not complete her training as a clinical psychologist. David's career rise, on the other hand, was meteoric. Ten years, seven house moves and four children later, he was made Director of a major company in Saudi Arabia.

This ushered in a period when Kay was the mainstay of the family: making sure the children were settled in schools, entertaining business contacts, doing all the myriad things that make a household run smoothly – even a well-appointed household like theirs, where help was on hand. David was less and less part of this day-to-day life, giving much of his time and energy to his career. She admired his success and appreciated the material comfort his work made possible. They had sex infrequently but – perhaps because of that – their love-making was usually passionate.

Time went by. The children grew up and started to live their own lives. Kay began to feel increasingly resentful, with a sense that she had sacrificed her life for David's career. One holiday weekend when they were at home together, all of their children away doing their own thing, she precipitated a major row, announced that she was leaving, and went back to England to stay with her sister. Back in the Home Counties, but unhappy and confused, she started seeing a counsellor.

David didn't know what had hit him. Within a month he was drinking heavily, had been prescribed Prozac and was finding work too much to cope with. He followed Kay to England, saw the company doctor and was signed off for a month. Kay asked him to go with her to see a couples counsellor, and he agreed, extending his leave of absence to three months so that they could sort out their problems.

When they started counselling together, Kay and David were almost in a state of shock at how bad things seemed to have got. To start with, each one took up an extreme position towards the other. For all his amazement at Kay's outburst, David had actually noticed that she hadn't seemed to be contented for some time. But he put it down to the menopause. He had thought that if she would only 'go and see the doctor and get some HRT' things would be back to normal. Later, he became angry with her at being the cause of so much disruption – and, as he thought, humiliation – in his working life. For her part, Kay could only see that she had given up her chance of a career to nurture the family. David's career had taken off, the children had taken off, too, and what was left for her?

Over the weeks, David and Kay worked hard to preserve a relationship they both now recognised they still valued very much. They loved and needed each other more than they had

realised and enough to take a good look at what was happening, to take responsibility for it, and to accept that changes had
to be made in order to start a new chapter. In speaking about
the family in which she herself had been brought up, Kay
realised with something of a shock that the model of a long-
suffering wife who does everything for her husband and
children was presented by her own mother. Her father, who
had been a sergeant in the armed forces, had often been posted
overseas during his career, and his wife had always 'held the
fort'. Subconsciously, Kay was following the same pattern and
she came to acknowledge that this was not something for
which David should take the blame. David's career may have
meant that he had not given as much time to the family as they
would have wanted, but at the same time it was the reason
why their life was very comfortable. Kay conceded that she
enjoyed all that their high standard of living offered her. A
sense of dissatisfaction had begun to creep in as the children
grew up, leaving Kay with an uncomfortable feeling that she
was no longer needed. Having tried to put her feelings into
words on several occasions without David appearing to take
her seriously, finally she blew her top in the row that preceded
her departure to England.

In his desperation, David cast about for straightforward
solutions to the problem. At work he solved problems all the
time, so why shouldn't he be able to sort out this one? If it was
the menopause, perhaps the counsellor could persuade Kay to
see her doctor? Kay was outraged at his oversimplification of
the case. He tried again: perhaps it was being away from her
family in England that was the problem. Right, he thought,
we'll buy a house in easy reach of Kay's sister, where there will
be opportunities for Kay to meet new friends and with a good
train service to London for the shops. But none of his solutions
for imposing a new life on Kay were going to work. As David
learned to listen, and Kay learned to give voice to her feelings,
they began to design their new life together.

Like many couples who have spent all their adult lives

together, raising a family, making a home, working for stability, David and Kay had gradually begun to walk on parallel paths, so to speak, each fulfilling their role and each making assumptions about the other. Neither had thought to check with the other that the course they were following was mutually satisfying.

It's easy to assume that because you are busy and success-ful achieving the mundane aims of your life the whole picture is rosy. It's a bit like painting a landscape by numbers, but get-ting so absorbed in filling in the different blues of the sky in the background that you forget to paint the green grass and vivid flowers that complete the scene. And when you take a couple of steps back and look at the canvas, you can see with a start that something very important is missing.

Filling in what feels like a frightening gap in your life isn't as straightforward as dabbing on the paint, as David and Kay found. But for them a crisis which had been terribly painful was a turning point which heralded a new era in their relation-ship. Each acknowledged the sacrifices made by the other: Kay may have given up the chance of a professional career, but David had lost out on the day-to-day contact with his family because he was working so hard to support them. They had both had their rewards, too: a beautiful home, pride in a suc-cessful career, the knowledge that they had given their chil-dren a good start in life.

After what had happened, neither felt that they could go back to the way things had been. Both knew that the time had come to make significant changes so that they could look forward to a fulfilling life together. They stayed in England. David scaled down his workload and Kay started to do voluntary work with handicapped children, something she'd been interested in since she was a student. Sometimes they go off to the country for a weekend together. There is an equilibrium to this life, matched by a new quality in the dialogue between them. A new thought-fulness, a new respect, comes out in the almost careful way in which they listen and talk to each other. They have found confidence in a future in which they will do their best to realise their potential as a couple.

KEEPING LOVE ALIVE

Kay and David have much in common with the rest of their generation. Like theirs did, most relationships begin with a short-lived period of heady romantic love. By the time a man and woman decide that they want to be united in marriage or commit themselves to each other in a permanent relationship, they will – it is hoped – not only have found out a great deal about each other, but also have talked about their hopes for the future. While the wedding itself might be a gloriously romantic event which both will look back on misty-eyed, they will find they need to be rather more clear-sighted in order to make a success of their life as a couple. If success means fulfilling shared expectations, that might well include buying a house, doing well at work, having children, taking a good holiday now and again. None of these are going to be achieved without effort, but whether or not you are aware of it, the endeavour is supported by the fact that lots of other people are doing exactly the same thing – indeed, daily life is full of little reminders that push you along the path. Think about it: your local newspapers are full of advertisements for houses and jobs; when you are at work, your boss will monitor how you're doing; there is less pressure within families these days for newlyweds to produce babies in the first few years; nevertheless once you have children a whole new range of imperatives make themselves felt. And as for choosing a holiday, the pressure is on the minute Christmas is over, with acres of newsprint and hours of television devoted to helping you to make up your mind.

But how often do you see a headline that asks you to focus on your personal life? When the alarm goes off in the morning, does it peal 'Remember to say "I love you" today'? When you get your bank statement, is there a little slip inside saying 'Invest in an affection account!'? When it's time to take the car for its MOT test, does the mechanic ask you how your tenderness rating's going?

No, nurturing your loved one is thought to be nobody's business but yours. With everything else that is going on in a busy, normal life – meeting the pressures to succeed and achieve, weighing up the constant inducements to buy this and that – it isn't any wonder that one day it dawns on you that some of the less tangible things you expected from your most important relationship have not been realised. To have done what you wanted in practical and material terms is satisfying, but it is not enough. You want to be partners in more and deeper ways than these. You don't just want to have a roof over your head and a little money in the bank: you want to be understood, respected, desired. You want to make each other laugh, introduce each other to new experiences, surprise each other now and again. If you reach a point where it seems as if this isn't happening, it doesn't mean that those expectations were unrealistic. It means you have started to think about what really matters. You have been given a chance to work for something worth fighting for.

NO PAIN, NO GAIN

For an encouragement to pursue physical beauty, Jane Fonda' s famous catch-phrase has a whiff of the puritan about it, and more than a grain of truth too, or it would not have so easily slipped into the language. Forgetting the pain involved in perspiring around the gym for the moment, let's acknowledge the emotional pain that's involved in any kind of life change.

We're all familiar with the ratings chart of causes of stress, showing that even supposedly positive changes can put pressure on individuals just as events such as divorce and death do.

Sometimes it can be helpful or comforting to see how other people have coped in equivalent situations – indeed, part of the fascination of the stress league table (see p.17) is the way it demonstrates that most of us find the same things difficult to endure. Some people seem to thrive on change; others prefer a quiet life, but whatever our personalities, there are some changes we as human beings cannot avoid – and notching up the birthdays is one of them. No one can claim that getting older took them by surprise. But if you feel positive about growing, rather than negative about growing old, then your experience of becoming older will be a positive one. This is one of life's happier self-fulfilling prophecies. Doing something about making the second part of your adulthood joyful isn't simply a case of accepting the inevitable; as the social historian Gail Sheehy has said, it's a career choice. Making a success of it depends on a number of factors, among which attitude is crucial.

You leave school, get a job, leave home, get married, have children, move house, get another job, someone in the family falls ill, someone loses their job, the children grow up and move on, someone marries and goes to live on the other side of the world, someone dies. These are the kinds of things we mean when we talk about 'the normal course of events': a combination of the rites of passage all human beings must go through and a few of the surprises life has up its sleeve. The people who cope best are those who, first and foremost, recognise them for what they are: normal.

In one sense life really is like a long journey, cliché though this may seem. On a real journey, of course you make sure certain things are in place before you hit the road – you fill the car with petrol, check the oil and tyres, look at the map and pack a picnic. As you start out on adult life, too, you make certain wise preparations: you make the best of your education, think about what job you might do and see if you can find it. You look for a suitable partner, you plan a family together and make a home. These are universal experiences: most people

Causes of stress

	Stress rating
Death of spouse or life partner	100
Divorce or separation	75
Major illness or injury	70
Loss of a job	70
Problems with the law/imprisonment	70
Death of someone close	60
Marital reconciliation	60
Retirement	60
Illness or injury in your close family	50
Marriage or moving in with partner	50
Moving house	50
Increase in arguments with partner	45
Large debt	45
New job	45
Accident or trauma	45
Changes at work	35
Caring for an elderly or sick relative	35
Problems with family or friends	35
Financial worries	35
Speaking in public	30
Changes in leisure activities	30
Children going away	30
Menopause	30
New relationship	30
Going on holiday	20
Family gatherings	20

Your vulnerability to stress-related illness is increased if your score of life events in the last six months is more than 280. Between 130 and 280 you are at moderate risk. If your life has been relatively uneventful recently your score will be under 130 and your risk of stress-related illness is low.

have dreams about falling in love, getting married and having a family. Some would even say that they feel a sense of destiny when they meet their life's partner – as if they really had 'arrived' somewhere.

On a journey, you might be held up by traffic or hear on the radio that the road ahead is flooded; an electrical fault might bring the car to a halt. Unwelcome, inconvenient, 'a pain' – but again, nothing out of the ordinary. Setbacks like these might justify a few deleted expletives, a change of route or calling out the roadside services. The kind of people who cope might resort to all or any of these strategies so that they can get moving again. Who wants to get stuck on the road?

It's the same in a relationship. As well as the changes you might actively seek, like having children or moving to a larger house, some time or another you are bound to face unexpected and less welcome events, too: redundancy, perhaps, or serious illness, or difficulties with teenage children. Every time something like this happens you have to change direction. Sometimes it is an almost imperceptible move, but at other times you have to slow down, or stop altogether, in order to make sense of what's happening. This is what happened to David and Kay, who – after travelling a long way on exactly the path they had agreed on – nevertheless had to screech to a halt when they came to a major crossroads. Lengthy renegotiations were required as they decided where to go next, and how fast, and with what resources.

DEALING WITH CHANGE

You will arrive at your own crossroads: it may not be dramatic or sudden, but the time will come when you have to ask yourself the question, 'What shall I do now?' It might well be because retirement age has arrived (maybe earlier than you had once expected); it might be because the children have left home for good; it might be because of the menopause; it might, sadly, be because your partner has died. It might not be a distinct 'event' such as any of these, but an almost intangible awareness that you yourself are changing subtly – and often the first indications are physical. Maybe mowing the grass takes a tiny bit longer than it used to; you need a bit more sleep, or a bit less; you put on a pound or two over Christmas and can't shift it as quickly as once you could.

By the time this point is reached, you have been through hundreds of changes in your life, and weathered them with varying degrees of success. Success is not really the point; the point is that you have experienced them and survived – even thrived. You are as expert at life as anyone is going to be. This life change is just the latest in the series. At this particular crossroads, however, there are two ways to go (and backwards isn't one of them).

Pause for thought

Everyone who reaches the age of fifty, whoever they are, has done a lot, has managed a lot of change.

Take a moment to think about the changes there have been in your life.

You left home?

Moved house?

Took a new job?

Became a parent?

Lost your mother or father?

Got divorced?

Had an operation?

Found a new partner?

Most of us don't like change. We may initially resist as if we have no experience of it.

Don't underestimate the skills you've gained in accommodating changes in your life.

Some couples and some individuals will be happy to put their feet up metaphorically, feeling they have earned the right to take things easy from now on. Conscious that they are entering a new era, they welcome the release from activity and hard work that it brings. Others, particularly perhaps those who have retired early, find they want to make the most of all the opportunities on offer – and that road has any number of inviting little alleyways leading off it.

Martin didn't do either of these things. At fifty-eight, he was made redundant by the engineering firm he had worked for ever since he had left the army in his early thirties. His redundancy pay-off was substantial, and he was as fit as a fiddle. His wife Carol had always taken care of the domestic side of things, and done it very well. Their two daughters were grown-up now and living at opposite ends of the country – one working in an arts centre in the North-East and the other in Devon, happily married to a farmer and expecting her third child. Martin's sense of self-worth took a severe knock when he was asked to leave the firm, and he desperately needed to feel as useful and important as he had always done at work. His pride prevented him from sharing with anyone, least of all Carol, how anxious he felt. And unused to that feeling, he had to find something to do – and he had to find it fast.

The solution was under his nose: home. A home needs running; an efficient home needs running with military precision (so he reasoned), and (with his training) he could do it much better than Carol. It started with the weekly shop. Carol's tried-and-tested method, which had the virtue of mixing business with pleasure, was to drive herself to the local supermarket every Friday morning and install herself in the cafeteria with a cup of coffee and a Danish pastry at her elbow while she wrote out the shopping list. Even with this supposed indulgence, the whole process only took just over an hour and she was back at home by half-past ten unpacking the cans and packets. Once in a while she forgot something she'd meant to buy – but it was never anything vital, and hey – don't we all?

This wasn't good enough for Martin. Within a month he had taken over the whole process, driving them both to Tesco's 'before the rush' with two shopping lists already neatly written out (he did one half of the store, she was supposed to do the other). He saw no need for a time-wasting break in the cafeteria when they could have coffee at home afterwards, while he usually read the sports page in the daily paper.

Carol's resistance to this change in her routine was half-hearted; she knew Martin must have been upset at losing his job and wanted to do what she could to ease the blow. But what happened over the next year was that she slowly relinquished her role as the one who took care of the house and home as her husband muscled in. One by one, Carol sacrificed small but important parts of her life which had given her pride and pleasure in order to bolster up Martin's bruised ego.

The more capable Martin appeared to be, the more pathetic Carol felt. She became lethargic. As she allowed herself to give up more and more responsibility for their domestic life to Martin, lethargy turned into depression. He willingly took on more and more. Indeed he took Carol's retreat into what amounted to illness in his stride, saying to concerned friends, 'Isn't it a good thing I'm at home, now that Carol isn't able to do much?' By choosing not to resist Martin's inexorable march towards complete control of their lives, Carol – having been capable and content – put herself in a position where the only justification for a life where she had no role to play was to make herself ill. It was a very sad situation. Their marriage continued, but it never recovered. As long as they had had fairly well-defined roles, their situation had offered them both a fair measure of contentment. But the disruption of the redundancy changed all that.

If you march forwards at the crossroads without changing direction, and without looking to the right and left, you could find yourself walking through a wasteland. If Martin had chosen to adapt to change rather than resisting it, and to look for ways in which to lead a different kind of life, it could have been tremendously rewarding for him and for Carol, too.

REALISTIC EXPECTATIONS

Sometimes a man who has been looking forward to retirement because, among other things, it means that he will be able to spend more time at home with his wife, finds to his dismay that his dearly beloved doesn't want him under her feet all day. He is made to feel unwelcome in the house, so he takes to leaving it for increasingly longer periods – which he spends playing bowls, or in the pub, the garage or the greenhouse.

His wife, too, has been looking forward to his retirement, to the changed pace of life, to spending more time together, but suddenly there's lunch to be made every day and unexpected disruption to a well-established domestic routine. 'A husband to hoover around,' as one friend put it. It's often not until we are in the throes of something new that we realise how attached we were to old ways of doing things. Irritation with the disruption of routine quickly communicates itself in these situations and to avoid the discord, a couple may find themselves unwittingly establishing a new routine in retirement that replicates the old one. Namely, spending many daytime hours apart, exactly the opposite of what each had looked forward to.

Not unusually, men in this situation find themselves berated both for being around and for absenting themselves, while their wives are accused of nagging inflexibility and devotion to domesticity. Out of such circumstances hostility can begin to grow.

Hostility finds a fertile ground in later-life relationships where one or both partners continue to behave as if nothing has changed, hanging on for all they're worth to a style of life that's had its day. The truth is, and it is true for all of us no matter what our circumstances, that things are not going to go on for ever as they have always done. An unwillingness to accept this is often based on a kind of fear that control of life's direction is slipping away. During the years of working hard to get on and to make a home and bring up a family, we often complain about the constraints placed on us by the working week and the school year. But these constraints aren't all bad: they give life a comforting rhythm and supporting structure. We are bound to miss them when they are gone, and miss them most acutely to begin with. Life, once so clearly defined, goes fuzzy round the edges.

Older people sometimes say that it feels as if they are at the mercy of events, as if someone else is controlling their fate. The paradox is that late adulthood may well be the first time in life that control over your life – so far as human beings can be said to have that power – has been in your own hands. It can feel wonderfully exciting and slightly terrifying all at the same time. All your life you have either been dependent on others or responsible for them. Now you can suit yourself. You can make choices. You can be a bit outrageous. It takes a bit of getting used to.

This may be the hardest part – making the transition from a life well ordered by outside influences to one where you are free to do your own thing. Making the transition as a couple has its own interesting twists, for the likelihood of two people being perfectly in step at this (or any other) time of life is more or less remote. Where both have jobs, one may retire months or years before the other. A man who's still deeply involved in his work may not be aware that the focus of life at home has taken a big shift now that the children have moved away. Acknowledging that things have changed, or are in the process of changing, is important. Then you have to find ways of dealing with change so that the experience is positive and liberating.

Chapter Two

IT'S UP TO YOU

Loving relationships develop and grow. When you enter a new phase in life, such as retirement, both partners need to adapt and to be flexible in order to make the most of what life has on offer. What is needed is accommodation and negotiation. Some couples are well practised in these skills; others – like Kay and David – have to acquire them. Those who refuse to try – like Martin and Carol – become strangers. An unwillingness to come to terms with the changes time brings, such as affects people like Martin, brings with it a refusal even to try to learn. In the case of Martin and Carol, not only did they became strangers to each other as their relationship stagnated, but Carol's health suffered too. You often hear people who are thinking of divorce say 'We've just grown apart,' as if growing apart is something that just happens and cannot be prevented.

TAKING CHARGE OF YOUR LIFE

A breakdown in sexual communication often forces couples to face the fact that they have allowed a distance to develop between them. During the initial history-taking which is a fundamental part of Relate's sex problems service, many couples realise with something of a shock that they actually avoid contact. Helen and Geoff never meant this to happen, but by the time they decided to see a sex therapist they had not made love for two years.

Helen and Geoff's courtship had been passionate when they first got together in their early thirties. Very much in love when they married, within five years they found themselves with a daughter and twin boys. The arrival of the twins coincided with a major promotion for Geoff, which catapulted them into a period of both parenting and career demands. Being mum and dad, or cook/cleaner and handyman/gardener left them little time at home to be just man and wife. They would hire a babysitter about once a month and go out to have a meal with couples in the same situation as themselves or to events – often connected with Geoff's work – where focusing on each other was not part of the programme. They kept their sexual relationship ticking over. They thought everything was fine.

Geoff was just fifty, Helen a little younger, when for the first time it looked as if they would have two weeks just to themselves while their teenage children were on various school trips. Disappointment struck when the holiday they booked for themselves fell through at the last minute; so they decided to take the time anyway and stay at home. They made a pact that it really would be a holiday – they wouldn't waste the time on DIY and gardening – they would have a good time.

And that's what they did, enjoying lazy days at home and a couple of outings to local beauty spots. It was wonderful, and in twelve days they made love more often than they had in the previous twelve months. Both of them were delighted to have recaptured the closeness and the passionate sexual relationship that had meant so much to them. They were determined to find time for each other in future.

Keeping their promise was much harder than they had thought. The boys came back and hit the house like a whirlwind. Their daughter was studying for A-levels and putting herself under a lot of pressure to succeed. Geoff's employers asked him to take on extra contracts. All the family came to stay at Christmas.

They were back on the treadmill, pedalling fast. Life slipped back into its old pattern, which once they had taken for granted but which now had something lacking. Their sexual contact dwindled, eventually dropping to zero. Each of them began to think that the other had lost interest in sex. They argued constantly. It was after a particularly horrible row that they decided to consult Relate, baffled that the legacy of their glorious holiday should be so much discontent.

Helen and Geoff described to the counsellor how their lives had been up to the holiday. They told a story of a not untypical family life in which husband and wife gave so much of their time and energy to others' needs that the need to nurture their own relationship got lost along the way. During their unexpected holiday they had recaptured not only the passion but also the intimacy of their first years together. It had been so wonderful that in the ensuing weeks Helen in particular had felt that nothing less would do – that if she couldn't have the kind of closeness that time to relax together had given them, she didn't want anything at all. Not knowing this, Geoff had interpreted her rejection of his affectionate overtures as a rejection of him, and had not pressed the issue. Both became increasingly miserable. It seemed as if they had had a taste of intimate possibilities only to have them snatched away. The disappointment both felt was fertile ground for rows and misunderstandings.

Their problem was twofold: finding the time in which they could recapture what they had experienced; and finding ways of sustaining the intimacy they had rediscovered within their day-to-day lives. It seemed that they had failed in their promise to set aside time for each other. It seemed as if, given all the demands on them, they could not make time together a real priority. But their love and desire for each other was still powerful – they had proved that, and they were relieved to be able to say so. If they had found the time to talk to a counsellor, then they could and would find more time in every-day life for each other.

In the context of the counselling sessions, Helen and Geoff

recognised that not only were they allowed to have time to be alone together, they really needed it, and that they owed it to themselves to find it. They talked about little ways in which they could remind each other of their needs, and as they put them into practice realised that – deeply satisfying as their sexual relationship was – there were many other expressions of affection and connection that could keep their intimate relationship strong. They remembered how, in the early days, they were always hugging each other; the simplest trans-actions would be marked by a kiss, a caress or an affectionate squeeze. It is not difficult for long-term married couples to let the small wordless signs of love fall into disuse. Helen and Geoff brought all of that back into their lives. They did not wait for another holiday before getting their act together again.

What Helen and Geoff learned opened their eyes to the opportunities for togetherness that were in front of them every day. Looking at life differently will stand them in good stead when the time comes for them to start the process of winding down.

TAKING THE SCENIC ROUTE

Robert Louis Stevenson hit on something when he said that 'to travel hopefully is a better thing than to arrive'. Living in a goal-oriented society carries the danger that many ordinary human endeavours become influenced by the ways of com-merce. Success in the world of work, for most people, now means being focused, watching the bottom line, seeing results – and being very busy indeed. Helen and Geoff were certainly busy and this was the sort of life that a couple called Jane and Ken had led as teachers.

When they both retired, Jane at fifty-eight and Ken a year later, they were determined that they would at last have lots of time together and time to pursue their interests. Ken couldn't wait to get started on restoring an old Morris Traveller he'd bought at auction, while Jane wanted to study history of art. As a teacher of French and Italian she had often taken troops of students on school trips to European cities. In those days there had never been time to do more than make perfunctory visits to the galleries and museums.

She began by making virtual visits to The Louvre on her new computer, and eventually 'walked' round a different museum every day, surfing the net for new leads. Ken, meanwhile, had his head under the bonnet of the old car. And when he wasn't there, he was cheering on the local football team, as well as sitting on the club committee (they'd been on at him to join for years). Jane followed suit by joining the local historical society, and happily let herself be talked into becoming social secretary – it seemed a shame to let her years of organising experience go to waste, and the society needed someone who had good fund-raising ideas. They were both living examples of active retirement, telling their son and daughter-in-law they couldn't understand how they'd ever had time to work!

Ken's heart attack when he was sixty-one pulled them up short. For the first time since retiring they stopped to think about what they were doing, and how much they were doing. One spring morning, a day or two after Ken came home from hospital, they sat in their kitchen with a pot of coffee, looking out at the daffodils coming up in the garden and trying to put it all into perspective. Far from being retired they had conspicuously over-stretched themselves, continuing the pattern of busy days spent working hard for good causes and completely forgetting their own real needs – as if their unwritten motto was: 'I'm busy, therefore I am.'

Although Ken's system had complained dramatically under the strain, he was undoubtedly on the mend. But they'd been given a fright. Over the coffee cups, they admitted to each other that they'd been afraid they would get bored doing nothing. Then they started to think about what – in spite of all the frantic activity – they actually hadn't done. It was a serious omission: they hadn't allowed themselves time to appreciate being together.

They didn't waste any more time, however. Jane and Ken made that quiet morning the first day of the rest of their lives; one of many when they had lazy breakfasts, reading to each other out of the newspapers, choosing something new to cook together for lunch, making love in the afternoon if they felt like it. They found a balance between the non-stop life they had been caught up in and the nothingness they feared. Jane still enjoys the historical society once a month, and Ken still supports the local team from the sidelines. But he sold the Morris, and put the proceeds towards a week in Paris. Jane – with Ken by her side – saw the Mona Lisa for real.

Pause for thought

Think for a moment about what it is that has drawn you to read this book.

Are you interested because you are getting older yourself?

Do you want to make more of life?

Have you already identified aspects of your own life in the couples described so far?

What aspects of their stories strike a chord with you?

Just pause here for a moment and let yourself reflect.

THAT WAS THEN, THIS IS NOW

It need not take a severe shock like a heart attack or a change in circumstances like losing your job to make you face whatever it is you fear about getting older. And facing those fears is a barrier that has to be broken through in order to find the positive advantages of second adulthood. Putting it baldly, getting older makes you aware of what you have given up. Your time of active parenting is over, and you may not have the prospect of becoming grandparents for a while; involvement in the workplace is coming to an end – and if the hoped-for promotion hasn't materialised by now, it probably never will; some of the dreams of youth may now be unattainable – or at least, less practical, if sailing single-handed around the world was what you always wanted. It's a common reaction to deny that these changes are happening. You may try to interfere in the lives of grown-up children, much to their frustration. Or you may pressurise them to produce grandchildren so that your lost parenting role does not have to be surrendered at all. Some of you will continue to buzz around just like you did at work – witness Jane and Ken. Some people will find it extremely difficult to come to terms with a diminution of vigour and become very depressed.

Thoughts of not being young any more, feelings of dissatisfaction or hopelessness, may creep up on you as you approach later life. Feelings like this cannot be ignored. Perhaps it is inevitable at a time of reappraisal to think in terms of what you have failed to do, of unrealised dreams and ambitions. You look back on your life and sometimes find it difficult to focus on what you have achieved – somehow you cannot help thinking about the things you have not done.

Marian was the youngest of four daughters. At sixteen she had started work as a clerical assistant in the local taxation office and had spent her whole career working in its various departments. She had refused all promotion that might have meant she needed to move away from home, content to live with her supportive but rather protective parents. Marian's major interest had been girl guiding and she was active in the guides throughout her twenties and thirties. Her social life revolved around guiding and most of her friends were fellow guiders.

At the age of nineteen she had been briefly engaged to Brian, who worked in the same office. The romance was chaste and short-lived and had ended abruptly when she discovered that Brian was two-timing her with another girl from work, who had become pregnant. Marian was devastated and moved departments to get away from the humiliation. Her parents had been against the match from the start and told her she was better off without Brian. Marian resolved never to get hurt again and settled into the safe territory of the devoted daughter, and the all-female environment of the Guide Association. She had never really been comfortable in the company of men, much preferring women's company. Her life became filled with work and guiding. She enjoyed being aunt to her sister's children and was happy enough, her only real ambition one day to be district commissioner for the area.

On her fortieth birthday her father, aged seventy-four, had a stroke. He lost his speech and his mobility and needed twenty-four-hour care. The prognosis was not good so Marian felt she had no choice but to withdraw from guiding for a few months to help her mother to look after him. But the months became years and everyone said it was only their continuous care that kept her father alive. Her mother got frailer and frailer and Marian never went back to guiding.

She looked after her parents for thirteen years, promising them when they got upset that they would never be put into a home as long as she was alive. She enjoyed being seen as the devoted daughter and there was purpose in her life. Over the years, however, she came to resent her sisters bitterly. Sisters who gave her little help and who always had other things to do. Marian didn't ask and they didn't offer. They visited, of course, but would never take over for a week while Marian took a break, the demands of their husbands and family taking precedence. In thirteen years Marian had five single weeks to herself while her parents had respite care in nursing homes. On the last occasion Marian was convinced that her parents had not been looked after properly and were very distressed by her absence. That was the end of respite care.

Marian had been forced to take early retirement at fifty-one when her mother had become bed-ridden and there were cutbacks in the community care available. Without work she became more and more short-tempered, fell out with her sisters by turns, argued with the neighbours about barking dogs and parked cars and generally felt that everyone was against her. Her bad temper distressed her mother particularly. On bad days Marian would wish her parents dead. She now bitterly regretted the decision to stay at home and be the dutiful daughter. Her mother should have insisted that she take promotion, that she should not give up guiding. She felt she had no life at all and had nothing to look forward to. She could only think of what she hadn't done and how little she had in her life.

When her parents died, within a week of each other, Marian was distraught. She blamed herself for not doing enough, for secretly wishing them dead. In the next couple of years, bereaved, exhausted and having lost her main purpose, Marian became more and more reclusive, taking little care of herself, the house or the little garden which had been such a source of pride. Far from feeling freed from the burden of care to take up a new life full of opportunities, she could only ruminate on what she didn't have and hadn't done. To start with, old friends tried to take her out of herself, but she would have none of it. Gradually they called less often and in time gave up. Marian was fifty-five but looked seventy. She was eventually treated for depression but wouldn't take the medication. Her world became smaller and smaller as she watched endless television and left the house as little as possible.

Being honest with yourself about feelings of regret means not only recognising that they exist, but also being realistic about their source. You have to take responsibility for your life rather than blaming others. Only in this way can you go on to make a realistic reassessment of the future. For example, you may feel that you have not fulfilled your potential because someone else was holding you back, when the truth is that you could never quite find the courage or strength to do the things you wanted. In this situation there is nothing to be gained by blaming another person. Your chance of 'making up for the past' lies in your own hands.

While the opportunity to do whatever it was you once wanted may have passed, there is still opportunity and time to achieve other goals, however modest. Finding new, realistic goals and setting out to reach them, can give you a new sense of self-respect. Your new goal need not be anything to do with past ambitions. The point is to find your true strengths and make the most of them. You may never have learned to swim; never travelled in an aeroplane. There is nothing to stop you setting yourself a target of swimming two lengths in the local pool or making the short flight to Dublin. If you do it now, the benefits will be far greater than simply making it to the deep end or stepping off the aircraft with a feeling of triumph.

Sometimes in order to create a more positive future it is necessary to move on from forces which have been negative. This might be so if you have been living with an abusive partner. But new does not always mean better; it can be destructive to force dramatic changes in your life, to detach yourself from what is familiar in an attempt to escape feelings of anxiety. Walking out on your family and your job will not make depression go away. It is more useful, in the long run, to try to work out what these painful feelings mean.

Depression can feel like a prison, and it is natural to want to get out of it. The psychologist Dorothy Rowe, who has written with great wisdom on the subject, has talked of the need to take care of yourself (something we often tell other people to do) in the most basic ways: making sure you eat well, getting enough sleep, taking some exercise and getting out in the fresh air. Each one of us can find something simple – the sight of trees by a river or the sound of inspiring music – which has the power to take us out of the circle of anxious thoughts.

Pause for thought

Think of three or four simple things that give you pleasure.

Is it a song that always makes you want to get to your feet and dance?

Is it a particular time of day when the view from your window or on a favourite walk is especially beautiful?

Is it taking a long soak in a hot bath in the middle of the afternoon?

Is it settling down with the family picture album and thinking about good times you have had?

Give yourself permission to enjoy these things.

Think about ways in which you can be sure you can have time to enjoy them.

GETTING A LIFE

As we get older, the sense of immortality we had when we were a child fades away. We become aware of our own mortality. Evidence of our physical ageing reminds us of it. The longer we live, the more likely it is that we will experience the death of others. When our parents die, the loss is profound. Mixed up with the sadness is a sense that now we are the 'older generation'. We are in the front line of the community of human beings facing death ourselves. It is unnerving when we read in the newspapers of the death of a celebrity who was born at about the same time as we were. We all know for certain that we must die, but we make very little preparation for it and do not care to be reminded of it.

Several theories have been put forward by scientists of ageing to explain why creatures (including humans) die. The idea that we all have to go some time to prevent overcrowding has been disproved. What now seems the most likely explanation is that, as Tom Kirkwood puts it in his fascinating study, *Time of Our Lives*, we are simply disposable, at least from our genes' point of view. To borrow Dr Kirkwood's anal- ogy, our maker has made a successful compromise between long-term durability and manufacturing costs. And if the longevity of the species is a measure of performance, the success of the design is proven: human beings can live to 122, according to the records. Only the Galapagos tortoise comes anywhere near, at 106 plus.

We know that night follows day and that the golden days of autumn lead to winter. We do not fear these inevitable events; we accept them and make provision for them. As human beings we find it far harder to come to terms with the other inevitable losses that, in the natural course of events, culminate in our own passing. But we have to try, because otherwise we are in danger of wasting the precious life we have. This is not to say that coping with the loss of our friends and family is easy to bear, far from it. It is crucially important, however, to acknowledge the loss and allow ourselves, or those close to us who have shared in the loss, to be sad, to be angry if we feel angry and to speak about what we are going through. It is going to be that much harder to contemplate one's own ending if we have not given ourselves the chance to deal adequately with our feelings of loss about others.

Unspoken feelings about the loss of a dear one can even have a physical effect. Ray and Margaret, seventy-two and sixty-eight respectively, were referred by Ray's GP to Relate. Ray had a number of health problems, including emphysema and a stomach ulcer. He was referred to a sex therapist because he had not been able to achieve an erection for four years. He and Margaret wanted to regain their sexual intimacy. This is what the therapist set out to help them to achieve, saying that she felt Ray's medical problems might make the aim of achieving erections again a bit ambitious.

Looking back on Ray and Margaret's life as a couple, it

became apparent that the loss of erections had followed on from a traumatic family event – the death of their son-in-law Donald in a road accident. At the time they had done all they could to support their daughter Tess and the grandchildren, but had done very little talking about what had happened. Ray in particular had felt that he had to soldier on and make himself available for Tess to lean on. Fatigue compounded with stress to undermine his health; loss of erectile function was part of that.

In the sessions with the counsellor they started to talk about what had happened. They began to feel free to talk about how much they missed Donald and how sad they were for the family he had left behind. There were tears, and they comforted each other. Ray admitted that part of him felt guilty for still being alive when someone so much younger had died so unnecessarily. It had been difficult for him to allow himself the pleasure of an active sex life. Instead of thinking of himself and Margaret, he used his energy to help Tess out – and to keep his own need for comfort firmly under wraps. Now they could both see that the time had come to give themselves some loving care.

Ray and Margaret were given relaxation exercises to do at home. They set aside plenty of time and at the beginning had a tape to listen to which helped them to get in the mood. The therapist explained how in a relaxed setting they could be intimate with each other by stroking and massaging without the need for anything else. Pretty soon, Ray found himself responding in a way he had almost forgotten. Over the weeks, he got more confidence in his ability to have an erection and more importantly, one he could use when he wanted to. Both of them were delighted with their much improved sexual relationship. The relaxation also helped Ray to manage his medical problems more effectively and Margaret saw to it that they did their relaxation exercises regardless of anything else.

DEATH OF A PARTNER

The death of a partner is thought to be the most stressful of all life events. When two people have been together for a very long time and have become very close, the loss is even greater. Sometimes people who have never lost a loved one fail to understand how long the process of grieving takes. The fact is that it is a long process, and a painful one, but it has to be gone through in order to carry on. Things will never be as they were before, but it is possible to reach a new kind of normality. The first reaction to the death is shock, leaving you numb, almost as if you are living in a dream. Often this is followed by a period of intense and confused feelings of anger, guilt and fear. The person you have lost may come to you in your dreams, only to slip away again as you desperately search for them. Later a feeling of utter bleakness may descend before the bereaved person begins to pick up the pieces again and edge towards a new, though different life. In that life sadness and desolation may return; but it becomes possible to accept the sadness as natural, just as death is natural. And with love and support the moments of loneliness grow fewer.

To help yourself to come to terms with your grief, allow yourself to cry when you want to and to talk about it when you can. Let yourself live at your own pace: don't take any notice of people who seem to think you should have got over it. Seek the company of people who are happy to accept you as you are and can be with you in an undemanding way. Try not to neglect your health: if you haven't much of an appetite, eat small amounts of nourishing food; get plenty of rest. When the time feels right, you can decide whether you want to make any changes and start to adapt to them. We don't forget those we have loved, but eventually we can let them go.

Death makes you sadder and wiser. It also brings people together in a way that joyful occasions rarely can. The experience of loss makes you better at understanding the experiences of others. It can open your eyes to the things in life which are really important; to the qualities in people that really matter.

LIVING IN THE MOMENT

Acknowledging the presence of death in life helps us to realise that we are alive. There are plenty of myths and fairy-tales about misguided characters who wished for immortality and were granted it, only to spend eternity in misery and regret. They had wished away the chance of valuing life and making the most of its every moment.

At the age of fifty-five, say, you can easily remember what was happening twelve years ago, when you were forty-three. Maybe you were living in a different house or even a different town. You might have had children at school who are now married. You might have had a memorable holiday that year or it might be the year you got a dog or your team won the cup. It seems like yesterday – no time at all. If that's so, then in no time at all you will be sixty-seven, with another set of experiences under your belt. What are you going to do with that precious time?

It is wonderful to have happy memories to look back on. It is good to plan for the future. It is essential to value the present. The chances are if you are reading this book that you have arrived at or will soon arrive at a stage in your life when you will have more leisure time than you used to. You will want to make the most of that gift of time; neither you nor your partner will want to waste it in hostility and frustration. Don't let the next twelve years of your life happen while you're busy doing something else. Life is not a rehearsal.

Chapter Three

CHANGING TIMES

Research conducted by R. Levenson and his colleagues in the early 1990s showed that for what they called 'middle-aged' couples, aged between forty and fifty, the three most important sources of pleasure (out of a total of sixteen topics) were: first, good times in the past, then other people and third, children or grandchildren. For what they called 'older' couples, aged between sixty and seventy years, children and grandchildren had become the most important, followed by good times in the past and holidays taken. Before considering the significance these findings, we need to take into consideration some of the life patterns that can be observed in the late twentieth century.

Broadly speaking, people are doing things later: staying on longer in higher education, getting married later and having children later. Figures gathered in the 1990s show that the average age at which women marry is twenty-six; for men the equivalent figure is twenty-eight, often after a period of cohabitation. Increasing numbers live together rather than marrying, in partnerships which do not produce children. According to figures published in 1997, the average age at which married women have their first child is just before their thirtieth birthday.

A generation or two ago, people aged sixty were very likely to have reached grandparenthood. If the statistics are anything to go by, they were enjoying it. But that source of pleasure is no longer something sixty-year-olds can rely on, because a significant proportion of our children are putting off having children of their own until much later. Some are electing not to have children at all.

Having said that, there are many more 'blended' families around these days than ever before, largely because people who are divorced often remarry, bringing their existing children into the new relationship and sometimes having more children with their new partners. Inevitably, some men and women aged fifty plus feature in this new picture of family life. Blended families present their own kinds of challenges to the people in them no matter what their ages, but an outcome peculiar to men and women (perhaps particularly men) in the older age group is the opportunity to become a parent again at an age when most of their contemporaries are waving their children goodbye, rejoicing in the birth of grandchildren, or just enjoying being free of parental responsibilities.

Many women now have children in their forties. Fewer give birth in their fifties, and those who do usually make it into the newspapers. It is becoming increasingly common for men to become fathers in their fifties, however, setting up interesting questions for the parent-child relationship. Children want their parents to be older and wiser than they are. As Dorothy Rowe said, as children 'we want them to be firmly there so that we can react against them and so be able to define ourselves, even if it is only in terms of "not like them"'. Parents who are very much older than their children may not be able to offer them all the security they need in one respect. One of the things children most fear is the death of their parents. Children of older parents work out at some point that their parents are going to die sooner rather than later. They are likely to be faced with coping with the death of a parent a good twenty or thirty years earlier than the rest of us will have to.

The age gap itself does not seem to have any disadvantages. In the same way that we learn not to expect our partners to supply our each and every need, so children accept their parents for what they are. Older dads may not have the energy of chaps in their twenties and thirties, but they are not past

SOURCES OF CONFLICT AND PLEASURE

Middle-aged couples (40–50 years)	**Older couples (60–70 years)**

Sources of Conflict

	Middle-aged	Older
1	Children	Communication
2	Money	Recreation
3	Communication	Money
4	Recreation	Children
5	Sex	Sex
6	In-laws	In-laws
7	Friends	Friends
8	Religion	Religion
9	Alcohol and drugs	Jealousy
10	Jealousy	Alcohol and drugs

Sources of Pleasure

	Middle-aged	Older
1	Good times in the past	Children and grandchildren
2	Other people	Good times in the past
3	Children or grandchildren	Vacations taken
4	Vacations taken	Things done together recently
5	Things done together recently	Other people
6	Silly and fun things	Plans for the future
7	Plans for the future	TV, radio and reading
8	TV, radio and reading	Casual and informal things
9	Casual and informal things	Silly and fun things
10	Accomplishments	Accomplishments
11	Views on issues	Politics and current events
12	Politics and current events	Views on issues
13	Things happening in town	Things happening in town
14	Family pets	Family pets
15	Things to do around the house	Things to do around the house
16	Dreams	Dreams

playing games and enjoying physical actitivies. And they have many other qualities to make up for running out of steam a bit earlier than they used to: patience, for one, and – especially if they have had children before – a kind of unflappability in the face of childhood ups and downs which first-time parents cannot aspire to.

Men who have been divorced often find that they have lost a network of friends – mostly couples – along with the marriage, and that the workplace becomes the arena in which their social life has an opportunity to get started again. This is when an older man might form a relationship with a younger woman. As more and more women return to work after divorce, once their family responsibilities are reduced, the same opportunities to make new social contacts are open to them.

Figures show that if a divorced man of over thirty-five marries a woman who has not herself been married before, he is most likely to choose one at least ten years younger than himself. And men over fifty-five may choose much younger women to marry, too. Sir Peter Hall was sixty when he married for the third time. His wife, Nicki, was then in her late twenties. They have a young daughter whose oldest step-brother is in his forties. In another less famous family the husband, in his mid-fifties, is married for the fourth time to a woman just ten years younger for whom it is a first – extremely happy – marriage. They have a child of six and an adopted child of three. He has grown-up children from earlier marriages and grandchildren the same age as his youngest children. A woman who is marrying for the second time in later life is just as likely to find a partner who is several years her junior and may, at fifty or more, find herself taking on a step-parenting role to his children when they visit at weekends – her own children having recently flown the nest.

The conventional pattern of what 'family' signifies has changed and is continuing to change. Blending two families presents particular challenges, which can be both eased and complicated when there is a blending of ages as well. The need to be clear about expectations and a willingness to negotiate and renegotiate are crucial.

Research in Europe seems to indicate that there is a correlation between the decline in marriage, the later age at which people are marrying and a drop in the birth rate. In Italy, for example, couples without children make up about 20 per cent of the total number of families. The average number of children per woman is about 1.2. The decrease in births has been so rapid in the last twenty years that in 1996 Italy became the only country in the world where the number of elderly people overtook the number of the young. This is likely to happen in the UK in 2008, when the number of pensioners is expected to overtake the number of children for the first time.

Another factor to be taken into consideration is that because people move away from home more readily than was once the case – perhaps to go to university, or because their job requires it – different generations of families are becoming more widely scattered.

The stage may be set for a raft of disappointed expectations. If you thought that your early retirement would be filled by helping out with a brood of grandchildren who lived just down the road, you may be disappointed. The reality is more likely to be no grandchildren, or none yet, or only one, who lives with his or her parents a good two hours' away by road – or even by air. As we become Europeans, as qualifications earned in one country become recognised across the continent, and as employment laws break through old barriers, young men and women looking for work will have much wider horizons than their parents did.

This can cause sadness, and it is important to acknowledge the sense of sadness while accepting the reality. Putting pressure on adult children to produce grandchildren is no answer. It can drive the generations apart and cause children to come into the world resented by their parents. And where there are grandchildren, putting pressure on sons and daughters-in-law to bring the children to visit more often, or hoping to occupy a more prominent place in their lives than they feel comfortable with, is frustrating for everyone. The rewards of the grandparent-grandchild relationship are enormous, but it cannot be forced. Better to make the most of the time you do have with grandchildren rather than waste it lamenting what you cannot control.

Women particularly sometimes look forward to the arrival of grandchildren because it compensates for the ending of the fertile years. But there is an added poignancy for couples who reach their fifties without having had children themselves. In Ann's case, for example, a confusion of feelings in her mid-fifties manifested itself as a loss of interest in sex. She and Bill, who was fifty-seven, had been happily married for twenty-two years, and it was only with the onset of the menopause five years previously that their sexual relationship began to decline. They were both puzzled and somewhat depressed by what was happening and eventually sought help from a sex therapist, while not really knowing what the therapist could do for them.

Rather than focusing on their sex life, the therapist began by taking a full history of every aspect of Ann and Bill's relationship, during which Ann revealed her sadness at never having had children. They had met in the Swinging Sixties and their relationship had taken off in the days of pop festivals, flower power and pleasure seeking. Their marriage and their sex life had been a great source of pleasure. Eventually they settled down, found themselves reasonable jobs and decided that they would like to raise a family. But Ann did not conceive. Series of tests showed no obvious reason for lack of fertility, and they had gone on hoping. The menopause was the final blow to Ann's hopes; as her hopes faded, so did her interest in sex. This did not mean she wanted the sexual side of her relationship with Bill to end, however. In fact, when asked what she hoped for from the therapy, Ann said that she wanted to feel sexual again.

The aim of the therapy was to grant her that wish; but it was a slow process. Talking to the therapist, Ann found herself expressing not just the disappointment of never having had a baby, but the anger, too. For his part, Bill said: 'I still have Ann. I look on the two of us as a family unit, even without children.' The therapist asked them to set aside special time for each other at home when they could give each other complete attention. They were given intimacy tasks to do during these times – touching, massaging and caressing each other – which helped them to grow in confidence. The time they devoted to each other, focusing on each other without thought of a 'goal' which they had to achieve, offered even more than that. They realised that this kind of close, intimate touching for its own sake was something they had both missed. They gave themselves the opportunity to tell each other how they felt – about each other, about their disappointment, and about how they wanted their life to be in the future. Bit by bit, being able to demonstrate their love for each other through touch brought about what they called 'the lifting of a great weight'. It was not only their sexual relationship which became more fulfilling; their friendship and respect for each other grew deeper, too.

When Levenson and his colleagues asked 'middle-aged' people what their second greatest source of pleasure was, the majority said 'other people'. Among 'older' couples, 'other people' came fifth. Other researchers have said that this trend fits in with what they have observed, that people become increasingly family-focused in old age. Having said that, as the boundaries of what constitute middle and old age begin to shift, it is likely that the focus on the family – with the implication that 'other people' are moved to the sidelines – will take place later and later. As this happens, received ideas about what is acceptable or suitable behaviour for someone of fifty, sixty, seventy or more change too – in fact the change is under way. And this is definitely a cause for rejoicing. It means that number nine on the list, 'silly and fun things', can rise up the charts, especially if they are silly 'things done together' (number four).

Having fun is something that older people are very good at. Take as evidence the popular television series, *Blind Date*. Once a week three twenty-something 'lucky lads' and three 'gorgeous girls' of similar age are tucked behind a screen as they answer three leading questions from a member of the opposite sex who then chooses one of them to take away on a trip. A week later, they come back to tell the audience how they got on – and what they really thought of each other. Once in a blue moon the pair hit it off and sit next to each other on the studio sofa with stars in their eyes. Nine times out of ten they haven't got a good word to say about each other and delight in parading each other's shortcomings to anyone who cares to listen.

Every so often *Blind Date* is handed over to the oldies – men and women in their sixties, seventies or eighties who like a challenge and a bit of fun. They dress up to the nines and behave quite outrageously. The questions and answers are frequently enough to make a maiden blush. Be that as it may, a week later when the fortunate pair come back from their adventure they are unfailingly enthusiastic about their trip and nice about each other – whether or not romance has blossomed. The contrast is between the bitter and the sweet: the bitterness of unrealistic expectations doomed to disappointment and the sweet rewards of knowing how to enjoy what life has to offer. And part of that knowledge seems to be that, as we get older, we can give ourselves permission to be a bit outrageous. It looks as if everyone is ready for it: this is the poem voted 'The Nation's Favourite' in 1997.

When I am an old woman I shall wear purple
With a red hat which doesn't go, and doesn't suit me,
And I shall spend my pension on brandy and summer
gloves
And satin sandals, and say we've no money for butter.

I shall sit down on the pavement when I'm tired
And gobble up samples in shops and press alarm bells
And run my stick along the public railings
And make up for the sobriety of my youth.
I shall go out in my slippers in the rain
And pick the flowers in other people's gardens
And learn to spit.

You can wear terrible shirts and grow more fat
And eat three pounds of sausages at a go
Or only bread and pickle for a week
And hoard pens and pencils and beermats and things in
      boxes.

But now we must have clothes that keep us dry
And pay our rent and not swear in the street
And set a good example to the children.
We must have friends to dinner and read the papers.

But maybe I ought to practise a little now?
So people who know me are not too shocked and surprised
When suddenly I am old, and start to wear purple.

The poem is by Jenny Joseph (born 1932), and she called it
'Warning'. Perhaps we should all write our own personal 'warning', and use it to list all the things we've been longing to do
but have been too busy, or too shy, or too well-behaved to
try. Skinny dipping? Hang-gliding? Chocolate sandwiches at
midnight? Learning Chinese? Buying a motorbike and a set of
leathers? Cooking Mexican food? Line dancing? A passionate
embrace in the kitchen? Why not, now that there's not likely to
be an unwelcome interruption from your children? How about
ripping up all the boring labour-saving euonymus in your garden and growing delphiniums – big ones – and floppy cabbage
roses? Once you get the hang of confounding everyone's expectations of you – including your own – it can be quite intoxicating.

Pause for thought

Let yourself have some fun reflecting on your 'outrageous' list.

You might like to write down, just for the pleasure of it, what your family and friends need to know about your intentions in later life.

Make a start here. Nothing is off limits . . . hang-gliding, scuba diving, breeding llamas, growing orchids.

It may be that you can only make a wish-list at this point but, if you let it, it could open up new horizons.

SUITING YOURSELF

Once powerful social taboos are fast disintegrating. There are some whose passing we might mourn. But there are others which had outstayed their welcome. The 'Mother's always right' authoritarian stance of our grandparents meant not only that the younger generation struggled to find their own identity, but that unnecessary barriers were placed between the generations. What, for example, would someone like Monica, aged sixty-one, have done if her daughter Ellie had felt unable to help her with her problem? A very common problem it was – stress incontinence, which had started more than twenty years before with the birth of her youngest son. Somehow or other she had coped with the odd 'leak' when coughing or laughing. When it started to happen at the climax of making love with her husband Robin, however, she did begin to worry. Monica became increasingly careful and restricted their sex lives to the man-on-top position in order to avoid these 'accidents'.

When Ellie had her first baby, she told her mother she was doing pelvic floor exercises every day to guard against stress incontinence – just the prompt Monica needed to say that, yes, she had a bit of a problem in that department. Ellie reminded her how to do the exercises (she had been told by the health visitor years ago, in fact, but had been too busy with the family to bother with them). With time and motivation, Monica began to do the exercises several times a day – they only took a few minutes – and gradually over the next few months began to feel much more in control. The effect on her sexual relationship was all to the good, as her former sense of adventure returned. (See page 194 for instructions on the exercises.)

Then there are independent women like Bobbie. As little as thirty years ago a single woman whose lover came to stay from time to time would have risked dirty looks from the neighbours. Now there are plenty of women like Bobbie, who – at seventy – likes it when her friend Jack stays for the weekend and likes it almost as much when he leaves on Monday morning. Much more than was ever the case in the past, women have the freedom to order their lives in a way that suits them, free from disapproving glances. The double standard is being chipped away.

In many families disapproval is used to reinforce rules and conventions. But as more and more younger people decide to live together rather than marry, for example, their parents surrender their disapproval, preferring to accept the lifestyle decisions of their offspring and to stay on good terms. It follows that if you tolerate such choices for the younger generation, it becomes acceptable for you, too. If, in later life, you embark on a second or third relationship you may not want all the trappings of marriage. Whether or not your first significant relationship was ended by divorce or death, it is not to devalue it to choose another kind of relationship in future. You may previously have had a distinctively caring or protective role which you no longer want to play; and that's fine – you can choose. As Bobbie says of Jack: 'I love having him in my life. I just don't want his feet under my table.'

Older men who are on their own either because of bereavement or divorce often find that friends and family work hard trying to match them up with someone they think is suitable. Sometimes that's fine and it has a happy ending. But just as often men in this situation find that they have difficulty in explaining to their well-meaning folk that, while they enjoy female company, they enjoy their independence too. They get fed up with other people's view of them as some sort of failure because they are still on their own. Living on your own is not the end of the world.

Alec enjoyed living on his own. At fifty-six, he had been divorced for ten years and had been going out with Grace, a widow two years older than him, for just over a year, when she began to say that she thought they ought to get married. Alec, on the other hand, thought the life they lived was fine just as it was. They saw each other at least two or three times a week, sometimes going out, sometimes just having a quiet evening at home, and often stayed over at each other's place for the night. They enjoyed each other's company and were very compatible sexually. Alec thought of them as a couple: he had no interest in any other women, but he did have a life of his own. There were several old (male) friends he liked to keep in touch with and once or twice a year he liked to go off on walking weekends alone. To him, Grace was a very important part of a good life.

Grace continued to press for something more. Alec felt strongly – in spite of Grace's assurances to the contrary – that if they were to marry she would want to place restrictions on him in order to make him spend much more of his time with her. He wanted to find a way of telling her that staying as they were was the best way to make both of them happy. When he suggested that they talked to a couples counsellor about the issue, Grace readily agreed.

Grace and Alec had two consultations with a counsellor. Grace heard Alec talk about his deep affection and real desire for her. She was left in no doubt about her importance in his life. She acknowledged his right to time on his own to pursue his own interests and maintain old friendships. The counsellor asked Grace to say something about what marriage meant to her, and as she talked it became clear that she had grown up thinking that, more than anything, marriage was a kind of fastness against the rest of the world; that when you took yourself a husband or a wife, you were placing on that person the expectation that you would be everything to each other. Her husband had died when they were both quite young – in their early thirties – after they had only been together four years, and she had not had the kind of life experiences that might have made her ideas a little less romantic, a little more realistic.

Grace still looked to the man in her life to meet all her needs. As long as she and Alec were to some extent independent of each other, she held back from claiming from him that he should fulfil those needs. But Alec had sensed that, if they did marry, she would begin to stake that claim and give in to a capacity for jealousy of his separate life. This, he knew, would begin to poison their relationship. Rather than let that happen, he wanted to keep it as it was. Even better, he cared for Grace enough to want her to be able to get from life all that she could, too.

Somewhere along the line Grace had accepted a blueprint for relationships between men and women that was stopping her from getting the most from the good relationship she actually had simply because it didn't fit the picture. Anxious about what she hadn't got, she was beginning to lose sight of what she had. Grace decided to go on seeing the counsellor for a little longer on her own, so that she could have the chance to explore what a greater sense of independence meant for her and what opportunities there were for her to find ways of meeting some of her needs in other ways. Alec was delighted not only that he had managed to retain her love, but to see Grace blossoming into a happier and more relaxed person.

GIVE AND TAKE

On the one hand, opportunity and freedom inviting us forward; on the other, ideas about appropriate behaviour holding us back. In the century which has seen radical redrawing of respective gender roles, it's not surprising that some of us feel confused. What has been happening, and what effect has it had?

To answer the second question first, we could start by looking at statistics for divorce in the UK in the last few decades. One of the most telling figures behind the statistics shows that as time goes by more and more divorces have been sought by women. At the same time, about half of the active workforce is female. So it would be fair to say that while women once looked upon marriage as the crowning achievement of their lives; while once upon a time being Mrs Somebody conferred social status on women which they could not achieve any other way; while once marriage was the only way in which a woman could achieve economic security – now, women who are deeply dissatisfied with their marriage or their husbands can free themselves from the bond. This is not to say that anyone undertakes divorce lightly or does not experience extreme pain; but the pejorative connotations of the label 'divorcee' have all but disappeared from the language. Now, so far from regarding being Mrs Anybody as the only sign of having arrived, many women cohabit with their chosen partners and never think of using his name to confer respectability on their condition. Indeed, many women who do marry still keep their own names, especially women who have carved out a career and whose maiden name is known to all their business contacts. And now, with the capacity to earn a living wage (if still not equal to what a man can earn), women are no longer completely financially dependent on their menfolk. In many households, the woman's wage is indispensable. Some women earn more than their partners. Many have achieved complete financial independence.

One of the most important advances of the century has been the provision of reliable contraception, enabling women to enjoy sex with their partners without the constant fear of unwanted pregnancy. This is only one of many advances in health care affecting women. Unlike our grandmothers, women of fifty today can look forward to an average of thirty more comparatively active years. The menopause might still be called 'the change', but it is emphatically not the end.

A combination of social, economic, political and cultural factors have combined to transform the status of women, and with it the nature of their relationships with men. If women do not need men to give them social or economic standing, what do they need them for? What do men feel they have to offer, and what to gain? These are undoubtedly pertinent questions for young men and women today, and they have reverberations for those of us who were growing up in the 1960s, not all of whom were caught up in the swing. Among this generation of ours are many women who place great value on marriage and what it has meant for them. But they are the ones who have also found themselves wanting more from marriage than stability and security. They have hoped for a depth and richness to their emotional lives, too, placing a demand on their partners which some men – who grew up thinking that fulfilling their duty as breadwinners would be enough – have found it difficult to meet.

In the struggle to redefine relationships between men and women, fairness has not always been in evidence. Professor Higgins' appeal has sometimes been turned on its head with the notion that if only 'a man could be more like a woman' everything would be all right. The danger is that this can simply give us a new set of not very helpful stereotypes. Hidebound thinking about the division between the sexes which paints all men as strong and silent and all women as soft and tender does not leave much space for men who are reflective, home-making types or for women who are high achievers at work or in sport.

In his book *Men are from Mars, Women are from Venus* John Gray has made some very interesting observations on these stereotypes. His thinking on the way men typically deal with problems resonates strongly with the experience of many couples. Rather than discussing the problem with his partner, John Gray says, a man will first work it out in his own head or go off to consult an expert. As he withdraws into silence or sticks his head in the paper, his wife – knowing instinctively that something is wrong – will ask what's up. She will get the answer 'Nothing'; an answer so thoroughly unsatisfactory that she will persist – 'What's the matter? Tell me what's wrong' – only succeeding in driving her husband deeper into his silent withdrawal. She pursues him vigorously, by now convinced that whatever is wrong must be something to do with her. But she cannot reach him, because metaphorically, he has retreated into 'his cave'.

By contrast, John Gray says that when a woman has a problem she is quick to share it with her partner, hoping for nothing more than a strong shoulder and a sympathetic ear. Partner, however, hears the problem as one he is being asked to solve and sets about finding a workmanlike solution, as the expert residing within him strides to the fore. She doesn't want an answer, however, she just wants to be heard. Neither of them realises that they are both missing the point. Feeling misunderstood and short-changed, in order to get what she needs, she may have to find a female friend with whom to talk the whole thing over. He feels unappreciated and frustrated. Their capacity to communicate effectively is continually undermined by the repeated pattern.

Throughout the life of our relationships we seek to be understood by our partners, but often fail to see that we have to find different ways of helping them to do so. Men go on behaving in the way they do. Women go on behaving in the way they do. A persistent pursuit-withdrawal pattern gets set

Pause for thought

It might help to give some thought to the typical pattern of behaviour that occurs between you and your partner when one or other of you has a problem or concern.

Do you recognise yourself or your partner in sections of this chapter?

Does your way of dealing with problems cause your partner concern?

up because couples fail to understand that each is dealing with their concerns in a different way. A husband will think that his way of sorting out the problem is the right one. When his wife starts to talk to him about a problem it feels as if he is being consulted. He thinks he is being expected to behave like an expert, so he expertly tries to find a solution to whatever it is she is talking about. His wife thinks that her way with problems is the right one – talking them over, giving them an airing. She presses her partner to respond to her wish to talk as she would herself – listening, being concerned, attending to her. But he cannot just listen any more than she can just problem-solve. His loving feelings propel him into 'expert' mode – giving what he perceives to be the most helpful response; her loving feelings propel her into the listening mode which she would find most helpful herself.

It is true that many men deal with difficult questions they need to resolve by temporarily 'checking out', that is to say mentally withdrawing from the scene. Sometimes they just go quiet. Sometimes they will lose themselves in unnecessary activity, such as mowing the lawn for the second time in a week. It is true that when they are upset, women are more likely to give way to their emotions and to want to run through the various aspects of whatever has happened with someone who is happy just to listen. If you think all men and women are like this, however, or that they are like this all of the time, you are placing limitations on how people are and how they might be in different circumstances or when given encouragement.

The big picture

One of the rewards of reaching the sixth decade and beyond is the ability to take a long perspective. In taking that view, we can perhaps see that the differences between men and women are to be celebrated as a source of mutual pleasure and comfort. We no longer believe that women are second-class citizens. Men no longer have to pretend to know everything about everything. Fortunately, equality does not mean sameness. Like Alec and Grace, we can think in terms of what we have to give each other and what we have to learn from each other, rather than just in terms of acting out traditional roles. And it is vital to go on learning and being willing to learn, in order to make the third age the best it can possibly be.

Chapter Four

IT AIN'T WHAT YOU SAY, IT'S THE WAY THAT YOU SAY IT

Setting aside time to talk and listen to each other may have to be a conscious decision. Some young couples where both partners are working are so used to organising many aspects of their lives that arranging to have time for each other doesn't feel that strange. It might be harder, however, to start to think in this way if you have been in a relationship for many years. Until it becomes part of the routine, it may feel a bit staged. Two people who have always been too busy to sit down and look at each other might feel uncomfortable and unnatural. Finding what feels like a suitable time is the first step – maybe there is a household routine that you always do together, like the washing up or putting the shopping away, which offers a good time for conversation – and it can develop from there. Some couples find long car journeys a good time to talk (as long as road conditions permit!).

Committing yourselves to finding the time is important. The next step is using it well, and barriers to useful communication can exist at a subconscious level. What you have absorbed about the 'right' way to behave – in families, and for men and women – can prevent you from being honest about your feelings or from sharing your joys and your disappointments. When you realize that the effects of these deep-seated ideas are harming your relationship, you might decide to do some painful unlearning.

Pause for thought

Think about your own relationship and identify a 'suitable time' in the day when it is best to talk.
Is it bedtime?
Sunday morning?
Over a drink in the pub?
When she/he is in a good mood?
If no time is a good time, do you want to do something about it?
Like it or not, you might need to think about how you can make it different.
Are you signalling clearly enough your need to talk?
Are you relying too much on telepathy in the hope that he or she will automatically know that you need to talk?

In chapter 9 the story of James and Kathryn provides an example of this in practice. James grew up in a boisterous family where, in spite of the best intentions, he was left longing for some quiet space that was just for him. Kathryn grew up in a quiet family where, in spite of the best intentions, she felt it was out of order to express negative feelings. Many men and women who grew up during the second world war and just afterwards were presented with models of behaviour that dictated, for example, that men kept a stiff upper lip when things went wrong. It was understood that women gossiped and chattered when they got together, but in mixed company they were expected to let the men do most of the talking.

Patterns of communicating according to gender are set very early in life. Little girls are expected to play with dolls or pretend to be keeping house: enclosed games that encourage intimate exchanges as they take care of their infant doll and make sure everything is all right – feeding them, washing them, keeping them warm. This is not a way in which females learn to assert their needs. By contrast little boys are expected to get out in the open air and kick a ball around or play at soldiers, with lots of shouting and physical aggression. This is not a way in which males learn to express their vulnerabilities. If a girl joined in the boys' games, she was called a tomboy. If a boy wanted to play house with the girls, he was called a cissy. When the lines between the different roles are so firmly drawn, it becomes difficult for one sex to take on the skills which the other is rapidly acquiring.

CONSEQUENCES

As time goes by, couples can get stuck in their stereotyped roles and the communication patterns that go with them. When there is a unexpected difference of opinion, they feel unhappy or resentful and begin to argue or retreat into hostile silence. They tend to focus on what the other person has done wrong or failed to do, without being aware that making an effort to communicate with each other more effectively about things can make a difference in itself. Think again about the case of Martin, the husband who took over his wife Carol's role, for example. A new phase in their lives which held opportunities was slowly wasted because he was unable to talk about the anxiety he experienced when made redundant. For her part, she was unable to speak about her own needs and to defend a way of life that she enjoyed.

When communication is working for a couple and the two of them are by turns really talking and really listening, the result is that each feels understood and appreciated. That is a good feeling. But it isn't just the feel-good factor that matters. Two individuals living in the real world are certain to have different points of view – but when they have opposite opinions, there is less likelihood that their arguments, however passionate, will be destructive if they are able to communicate. If one individual respects the other's right to a particular point of view, there is a greater likelihood that their own integrity will be respected.

We have probably all had the experience of feeling that we are not being listened to. It is bad enough when a shop assistant or waiter fails to bring you what you have ordered because they weren't paying attention. How much worse is it if your attempts to speak to your partner about something important fail to get through? While you can tell when it is happening to you, it takes a higher degree of self-awareness to know when you are doing it to someone else. You may only be half-listening – keeping one eye on the TV while your partner is trying to tell you something, for example. You may finish your partner's sentence instead of letting him or her find their own words. You might think, when your partner picks up the thread of an earlier discussion, 'Oh, I know where this is going', and make assumptions about what is going to be said as well as what is behind the words.

Pause for thought

What are your feelings when you are not listened to?
Frustration? Annoyance? A sense of *déjà vu*?
Have you given up trying to be heard?
Have you thought that the same might be true of your
  partner?
Food for thought?

Unwillingness to get drawn into a conversation about difficult or emotive subjects can mean that when one partner tries to talk about them, the other becomes critical or dismissive, ridicules the other or, worse still, simply switches off – the stonewall technique. The short-term gains of not listening are that a discussion that demands attention has been avoided and you have let yourself off the hook. The long-term effects are that an opportunity to deal with an issue that sooner or later will have to be dealt with has been lost, and with it has gone a chance to be appreciated by your partner for taking the trouble to respect his or her point of view or to be taken into their confidence. If they have been summoning up the courage to talk about something they find difficult, receiving any of the above reactions from you will ensure that they won't try again for some time. And that is not a gain, for it means you are drifting apart as the days tick by.

Angus and Sally were casually introduced by a mutual friend, who had known them both for years in different circles. A year went by before their paths crossed again, during which Angus and his wife had started divorce proceedings. The break-up of his family had hit him hard and he was doing his best to keep contact with his teenage children. As they now lived with his ex-wife and her new partner and Angus often had to travel abroad on business, this took some organising. When he and Sally started a friendship, which soon developed into a love affair, the fact that they lived in different parts of the country didn't seem to be too much of a problem. There were other demands on their time: both had work to do, and Sally had a teenage son of her own. They did not want to be living in each other's pockets. Part of the thrill of a new love affair was the passion of meeting again after being separated.

Soon a routine was established. Angus would visit Sally during the week, sometimes twice, and spend every weekend with his children over a hundred miles away. Occasionally he would invite Sally and her son to visit – for his 50th birthday lunch, for example. It was shortly after this event that Sally was aware of a distinct chill in his behaviour. In subsequent telephone conversations she tried to get to the bottom of it, but to no avail and eventually he thawed out. This happened on several later occasions. Now frustrated and angry, Sally issued a low-level ultimatum. Up with this she would not put.

Sally had been an only child of a distant, kindly father and a mother whose customary affection was sometimes turned off for no apparent reason. She grew up with a horror of these punishing silences and struggled in all her relationships not to repeat a pattern which had seemed so destructive. By the time she and

Angus got together, Sally had become a very independent character who didn't mince words. Angus acknowledged that he could be 'rather elusive' and said, somewhat reluctantly, that he would try not to shut himself off in this way in future – adding with a sheepish grin that he wasn't making any promises.

And in fact the effort was beyond him. The more it happened – and Sally never found out what the problems were – the more she found that the physical distance between them became a problem too. She reasoned that if they could be together more at weekends, when they could relax together, they would have a better chance of bridging the gap. But Angus, fiercely protective of his time with his children, was unwilling to give any of it up.

He did not want to give Sally up either. The last years of his marriage had been bleak, and Sally had brought love back into his life. The trouble was that as well as being affectionate and sociable, she had little hesitation in saying what she thought – and this kind of behaviour was quite at odds with what Angus thought he knew about women. His ex-wife had never said a word about being unhappy, but just announced out of the blue that she had fallen in love with someone else and was leaving. His mother managed all through her married life to give the impression that her husband ruled the roost, while quietly taking charge of everything herself. Women as people to be negotiated with had not been part of Angus's experience.

Matters came to a head one winter weekend when Sally, her son now away from home at college, invited some of her friends over for Sunday lunch. She asked Angus too – not only because she wanted them to be together as a couple, but also because she thought his agreeing to come would be a gesture she would greatly value. It would mean he was willing to give her the attention she had been asking for. He offered a compromise, saying that he would drive over at the end of his time with his daughter (the two older children had by now left home). Sally was on the brink of telling him not to bother, but her nerve failed and she said okay.

It was early evening when Angus arrived. All the guests had gone and the plates and glasses had been washed up and put away. Sally was too tired to do much more than lounge on the sofa with the Sunday papers, so that when Angus turned up expecting a warm welcome, it was not forthcoming. Barely polite to start with, Sally quickly launched into an attack, saying she felt Angus attached no real importance to their relationship. If they were a couple, how was it she did so much on her own? If being close to each other really mattered, why would he withdraw and sulk for days on end? Sally's only answer was the banging of the front door as Angus walked out.

She tried to call him several times in the ensuing weeks, but always got the answering machine at home and his secretary at work. She felt wretched. A month went by before Angus himself telephoned, hoping that things had blown over and they could get back to their former pattern. Much as she had missed Angus, however, Sally did not want to go backwards. Angus said he really loved her, but couldn't see how he could make more time for her. To Sally, being given more of his time and, therefore, his attention had become all-important. Without that, there was no point in going on. She said goodbye.

Not only did Sally never find out what it was that sparked off the periodic silences; she never worked out why her attempts to penetrate them always came to grief.

KNOWING YOURSELF

Since ancient times there have been attempts to pigeon-hole people into types. In Shakespeare's day the ideas of the Greeks still held sway, and people thought of themselves as having one of four 'temperaments' depending on which of the four elements – earth, air, fire and water – was dominant in their make-up. And still today people who read their horoscopes can say whether they are a 'fire sign' or an 'earth sign'. However cynical you might be about the value of horoscopes, there is an

Pause for thought

By now you will have gathered that effective ways of
communicating are vital in any relationship, and that
we develop our own methods.

How do you communicate your ideas, thoughts, feelings,
concerns?

What words would you typically use to tell someone else
about your current self?

Would you say
'I feel I'd be unhappy about . . .'
'I think I'd be unhappy about . . .'
'I believe I'd be unhappy about . . .'
'I sense I'd be unhappy about . . .'

What would your partner's pattern, be, for example, if you
are a 'feeler' and he or she is a 'thinker'? What impact,
if any, do you find this has on your conversations?

Might it explain how, on occasion, you are at cross
purposes?

Doesn't look much of a difference until the communication
patterns start to 'miss' each other and confusion and
bewilderment sets in.

Then is the exact time to recognise difference, value and
own it and work together to understand each other's
different way of seeing the world. It is not a time to
see the relationship as a battle to be won but rather a
discussion to be had.

Think about it.

element of truth in the idea of different temperaments. People
can be short-tempered and passionate (fire); cool and phleg-
matic (water); prone to melancholy and introspective (earth) or
mercurial and imaginative (air). These days we know better
than to believe that each person is either one 'type' – we

human beings are much more complex than that. We also know that in order to make life more rewarding, we can learn to manage our personality traits rather than falling victim to them. We do this, for example, when we learn to overcome shyness or to be less aggressive.

The very popularity of horoscopes shows that people are interested in what type they might be. To put it another way, people want to understand themselves better. The way in which we communicate with each other provides some very useful clues to the way we think: our mindset reveals itself in the way we speak. When they have got to make a decision about something, people who are considered and reflective will take time to make their choice and do lots of 'research' before they reach that point. They will delay the moment of truth by saying: 'I'll have to think about that . . .' or 'I'll just look around at what's on offer. . .' or 'Maybe we should look into . . .'. People who are instinctive and spontaneous won't want to go through all that and will make positive statements such as 'I like this one'; 'I'll take it'; 'Let's go there'.

In relationships, these different styles of talking and the thinking or feeling processes behind them can be a source of friction or of satisfaction. Opposites attract because they have the potential to complement each other. If you think back to the different qualities that attracted you to your partner, you may find that his or her more cautious approach to the world gave you a sense of security. If you are the more spontaneous and instinctive one, at some level you believed that they would be able to save you from rash decisions. On the other side of the coin, your partner might have valued that very spontaneity of yours, believing that it would bring sparkle and surprise into his or her life to balance their steady and sober side.

There are bound to have been times since then when the things that attracted you at first began to drive you mad. You might have said to yourself (or to your partner) 'Why do you have to go at everything like a bull at a gate?' when his or her impulsiveness has got you into a bit of trouble. Or, 'If you can't

make your mind up I'm going to explode!' when you have
spent what feels like an eternity trying to choose wallpaper or
where to go on holiday.

These moments of friction don't have to become a problem.
They can be like the little sparks in a car's engine that keep
it running. No spark, no movement. They make the other
person see that perhaps they've let their impulsive or cautious
side get the better of them. They create an opportunity to
laugh together, to appreciate each other and move forward
together. It can happen this way if you see your differing
natures and your differing ways of communicating as comple-
mentary. Neither is right, neither is wrong. There are two
truths in any relationship, and each person has a right to
express their truth.

These moments of friction become a problem if underneath
them each harbours the belief that only their way of doing
things is right; if this becomes a kind of power struggle, a
means of asserting one person's rights over the other. Then, an
exasperated outburst which could end up with a giggle and a
cuddle ends up with seething resentment and a brief fillip to
false pride. What could have been an occasion for getting
closer actually puts a greater distance between you. Better to
come to an amicable compromise about the wallpaper and
close the book than foist one person's choice on the other
(who will probably never be able to feel happy in the newly
decorated room anyway).

STAMP COLLECTING

Many people reading this book will remember collecting 'Green
Shield' stamps from garages, supermarkets and ironmongers
in the late 1960s and early 1970s. When you purchased petrol
or groceries or paint stripper you were given stamps to stick in
a special stamp book, until you had sufficient to get a free
set of glasses, pair of pillowcases, or – if you had enough – a

transistor radio. It was 'something for nothing'. And most of us enjoyed the ritual of sticking the stamps into the Green Shield stamp book after a shopping trip.

The deal was that the stamps had to be stuck in the book in order to collect the so-called freebies. Even though we knew then what we know now, that nothing was truly free, the ritual of collecting the stamps was part of the pleasure. We knew that one day we would be cashing them in. In thinking about managing the ups and downs of our relationships we might hold this analogy in mind.

When two people first meet and make the first moves towards becoming a couple, they find out an awful lot about each other. The most important exchanges of information take place in numberless conversations. In these conversations they share ideas about their hopes and aspirations, their standards of behaviour, the values they hold dear in life. What comes out in these conversations enriches the relationship and establishes the base line of what is acceptable within it. Over the months/years that these exchanges take place, each learns about the other's character. He might discover, for example, that while she is sometimes quietly content when they are together, she can also be the life and soul of a party. She realises that he is someone who always means what he says; she can rely on him. They like these qualities in each other. The relationship continues and they get married.

In their married life, there will inevitably be disruptions. Things will happen, or not happen, which will have the effect of putting a little dent in the smooth running of the relationship. Silly things, some of them: he seems to be incapable of keeping track of his socks, and regularly shouts down the stairs asking where they are. And every time he does she says to herself, 'If he does that again I'll blow my top.' But every time she just shouts back up to him, 'They're in the airing cupboard, where they always are!' She seems to be incapable of getting anywhere on time, and regularly causes him nail-biting hours of worry when he's left waiting to pick her up at the park-and-ride on the edge of town. Every time he thinks to himself, 'If she does this one more time she can bloody well walk home.' But every time, when she gets into the car full of chatter about her shopping, he just mumbles, 'Fine time to turn up, this is' and drives home.

Every time something like this happens, each of them silently sticks a stamp in their little book of grievances. They may not even know they are doing it, but they are. And just like a book of savings stamps, one of these days they will have to be cashed in. Eventually, after a series of the usual little unremarked annoyances, when the little book of stamps is almost full, one of them goes too far. He or she does something that significantly disappoints their partner's expectations of what is acceptable. It may not be to do with clean socks or any other kind of laundry; it may not be bad timekeeping. In fact it almost certainly won't be any of these things, and its lack of connection to previous small offences will make the impact of the sudden eruption even more powerful.

The book of stamps is cashed in. The offending party gets the book thrown at them, in fact, and doesn't quite know what's hit them. It's not a pleasant experience. But the one who has cashed in their stamps feels much better now that they've let off all that steam and have relieved all the stress that has been building up for weeks or more. And now that that's over, they can apologise for the outburst and start filling up a new book of stamps. The pattern of saving up petty grievances to be spilled out in one huge explosion will endlessly repeat itself, causing increasing stress and distress to both partners.

Anita and Tony had always rowed a lot in their relationship. The rows were a constant source of concern to them. They seemed to come out of the blue but on a seemingly regular basis. They knew that they cared a lot about each other and always eventually kissed and made up after a row. But deep down they were worried that at some point one or other of them would have had enough and there would be a break-up.

Despite the rows, Anita and Tony were seen as having a

good life, a lovely home and three successful grown-up children. When asked, they would say that they liked the same things, enjoyed each other's company and had a good time on their holidays together. Their active social life was shared with a group of long-standing friends who understood their up-and-down pattern and accepted it as 'how it was' for Anita and Tony.

Their rows never really seemed to clear the air. As they got older the arguments seemed to come out of nowhere – like the flare-up they had at a barbecue at a friend's place one evening. It had been what they both described as 'a perfect day in the garden'. This time they both realised they needed to get to grips with whatever it was that was causing such friction.

Tony contacted Relate for an appointment, much to Anita's surprise, consternation and relief. In the two weeks that they waited for their appointment things were, as Anita put it 'a bit chilly'. They nevertheless did a lot of private thinking in that time and were ready to do some serious sorting out when they arrived for their appointment.

Anita and Tony were well matched. They had met when they were still at school and were seen by their respective families as right for each other. The families were very similar. Both fathers worked in the engineering business – toolmakers in different firms – and both mothers stayed at home.

Keeping everything in apple-pie order was the order of the day in both families. Mother saw to it that father, who worked hard, came home to peace and quiet. Father bolstered mother, who worked just as hard, in disciplining the children so that they were well behaved and respected authority.

Whenever Anita came home from school with a problem or unexpectingly needing money for a school trip, her mother would say, 'Don't bother your dad; we'll sort it out.' And of course her mum did. And later, when she was a teenager and went shopping for clothes with her mum, she learnt that her dad didn't always get to know how much they had spent when he asked. Mum always managed the finances and Anita learnt that 'You only told men so much'. She learnt to edit what she shared with her dad. More significantly, however, she learnt to edit the expression of her feelings and needs.

Tony used to go fishing with his father when he was a lad. He gradually picked up his father's philosophy about women on these trips and learnt that as far as his dad was concerned it was best to keep your worries to yourself when it came to wives, because they only worried unnecessarily.

And so Anita and Tony came into their marriage armed with similar beliefs about confiding fully in each other. Whenever one of them behaved in a way that left the other disappointed, upset or feeling hard done by, instead of sorting it there and then, they only let the other know some of their feelings and began the inevitable collecting of 'grudge stamps'. Over the weeks and months un-dealt-with hurts and rejections would be collected in this way until the 'book' was full enough to be cashed in. And, of course, for Anita and Tony cashing-in time always involved a big row.

Afterwards, there would be a swift reconciliation, tears and flowers, which papered nicely over the cracks but never really got to grips with the fundamental problem. Anita and Tony needed to learn to deal with their reluctance to tackle things that upset them as they happened, not months later when reliable memory of the events that upset them was lost. The pattern that had worked fifty years earlier for their parents belonged to a past generation and had no place in their marriage.

In their counselling sessions over three months they began to realise that in choosing not to deal, at the time, with the everyday gripes and rubbing points of their relationship, they were likely to have more significant rows at a later date. It was much better in the long term to say, 'I thought we'd agreed last month that I would pay the window cleaner when he came for his money,' than to harbour brassed-off feelings because it hadn't happened like that.

It took time. Anita and Tony realised that old habits died

hard, and that they needed to be each other's watchdogs. They still had a good set-to occasionally but at least they now knew why and could agree to do something about it.

Pause for thought

To reflect productively on the following questions, you need to be really honest with yourself. Your responses are likely to be the same as those of thousands of others.

Do you save up small grievances in your relationship, like Anita and Tony?

Do you find it difficult to say what you feel at the time?

Is that how it is for members of your original family?

Do they behave like you do when faced with upset?

Now be honest and ask yourself how many small 'stamps' you have stuck in the stamp book of your particular relationship in the past month.

And perhaps more importantly – do you recognise the behaviour that guarantees you'll be able to cash them in?

Unhealthy patterns like this will go on unless both partners decide to stop it by finding out why it's happening and agreeing that it is not doing either of them any good. The reason is often to be found in the communication blueprint that was taken on by one or both of them in early childhood. As well as the socially acceptable modes of behaviour that men and women have to deal with, there are particular communication systems at work in different families. As children we will have observed the way our parents behaved and we will quickly have worked out what we needed to do to fit in with our family's way of doing things.

If, for example, you got used to hearing your mother say, 'Don't tell your father' about literally anything that she thought might upset him, you might have got the message that it's best not to deal with little problems as they crop up. A little voice inside will have told you not to make trouble. You told yourself it's not worth making a fuss. You believed you must keep it to yourself if someone hurts your feelings or lets you down. Or you might have been given a blueprint that said if you want anybody to take notice of you, you have to fight your corner no matter what. You come to believe that you always have to speak first and speak loudest to justify your existence. You may have been in a family where silence was part of the system. Your mother or father might have dealt with their differences not by discussing them, but by distancing themselves from each other. Having taken up opposing positions they then communicated through others, drawing the children helplessly into the game. It's in these situations that you might have heard your mother say to you, 'Ask your father if he wants some marmalade' or your father say to you, 'Tell your mother I'll be home late tonight.'

Communication systems in families are very powerful. As a child, you did not dare to challenge them, and having had few opportunities to compare the details of your families' lives with

---

Pause for thought

Think back to your family of origin and try to remember how they dealt with disagreements and upsets.

Were they all tidied away and not spoken about for fear of upsetting someone?

Did you learn to keep quiet and not upset people – your mum, your dad, your gran?

Have you operated like that with your own family?

Do you follow the same pattern now?

It may be difficult to reflect on these questions but it may be a key to the changes you want to make.

others, you probably didn't even know that some people did things differently. Growing up in the 1950s, much of your social interaction would have been within the extended family, with aunts and uncles who by and large felt as your parents did. So by the time you reached your teenage years, you had thoroughly absorbed a set of rules about what could be spoken about and what was kept quiet.

When you got to your adult life, you started to think about finding a partner and settling down. In the search for a partner, you met someone you liked and eventually met their family. That family's way of behaving with each other might have been very different from what you were used to. If you were used to a quiet and measured way of doing things and found yourself in a houseful of people who seemed to be talking non-stop at the tops of their voices all the time, you might have found it wonderfully exciting or absolutely terrifying. If, on the other hand, you were used to having to make a bit of a noise to get yourself heard at home, being introduced to a family of softly spoken, patient people might have felt calm and restful. At the same time that you were taking the measure of the family, you and your potential partner would have been having the sort of conversations with each other that helped you to find out whether or not you were right for each other.

For those of us who are now fifty or sixty that time of emerging from the family fold will have more or less coincided with the 1960s. You were in your late teens and twenties, and beginning to observe the way other people lived with and treated each other at a time when the whole idea of 'making a statement' came into being. As often as not, however, this statement did not express itself in conversation. Such words as were current were the lyrics of pop or protest songs. 'Statements' were made most powerfully in visual images: how you looked was very much more important than what you said. The style of the 1960s was brash and vivid. Just ten years before you had been squinting at the Coronation on a tiny black and white television set. Now you were dazzling everybody with your psychedelic gear. The uniform made the statement for you.

In those days, there was a shorthand way of talking to each other and being understood. ('Are you dancing?'; 'Who's asking?'; 'I'm asking'; 'I'm dancing' − a typical romantic encounter on the local dance floor.) Conversations like that may serve a purpose at the time, but if you really want to communicate thirty years on, this is no longer good enough. Effective communication is required and this takes effort and hard work.

When people say you've got to put something into a relationship to make it work, this is the kind of work they mean. Communication takes effort and in particular it takes real effort to listen properly. You have to focus your attention on the speaker, resisting the temptation to interrupt. You have to think about what they have said before you make a response. Only if you can do this will your partner feel that they can trust you with their most private thoughts and feelings.

Pause for thought

Are you a good listener?

Are there times when you find yourself at cross purposes with others?

Be honest. Did you really just not hear what they were saying?

Were you preoccupied with preparing what you were going to say next?

Do you find yourself interrupting people half-way through their sentence?

Do you realise that these questions are probably the hardest you will have to answer?

The courage to speak

Good listening takes real effort, and by comparison talking might seem easy; but unhelpful habits and ideas about what is appropriate behaviour can still get in the way.

Any of the influences we have looked at or a combination of them have made it very difficult for some members of our generation to speak about anything other than the most mundane and superficial matters. Saying 'I love you' and 'I hate it when you do that' are equally hard to say because expressions of emotion make them feel embarrassed. On the one hand there are chaps for whom being a faithful husband and provider is their way of expressing a love they cannot put into words. For some wives this is enough. But for others, there is a longing and disappointment that feelings cannot be addressed. And there are also women who brush off their partners' romantic overtures as nonsense and just want to be left to get the dinner on the table. Husbands whose demonstrations of affection are pushed away can feel a mounting sense of rejection and disapproval.

Chapter Five

HAVE I MADE MYSELF CLEAR?

It has been said that England and America are two nations divided by a single language, and it sometimes seems that in couple relationships, too, using what purports to be the same language only results in confusion. After all, language is a tool. If we are going to use words properly, we are well advised to choose and use them carefully. This doesn't mean that we all have to be literary high-fliers – but if what we say is not having the effect we expected, it becomes necessary to give some thought to how we are saying it. We all know the old joke about English people thinking they can make themselves understood abroad by talking very loudly, when actually it's not shouting that is going to aid comprehension, but consulting the phrase book. Similarly, if you don't feel that you are 'getting through' to your partner, saying the same old thing the same old way isn't going to cause a breakthrough.

If you and your partner have been together for some time, it is almost inevitable that you will make assumptions about how the other person is feeling. There are occasions when this can be positively helpful. A man who knows that his wife needs eight hours' sleep every night to function will make sure they have a quiet evening at home if the next day she has an important meeting at work or an early start with the children. If he has never noticed this, he might fix up an evening out and wonder why his wife is considerably less than keen. A woman whose husband travels abroad on business might know that he is badly affected by jet lag and that it's best to let him relax for the first day or two after getting home. If she has never noticed this, she might launch into a catalogue of domestic problems the minute he walks in the door or invite six people round for dinner – and wonder why he hits the roof.

The danger arises when couples who have been together for a considerable length of time draw negative assumptions about the other's behaviour, and give voice to their conclusions in a way that comes out like an accusation. When this happens, it is that much harder for the person to change their behaviour in a way that doesn't make them feel as if they have been forced to surrender. Here is an example. Mollie's husband Jim took up golf in his late thirties, when some of his workmates introduced him to the game. It became a regular fixture that he would spend every Sunday morning on the golf course, arriving home in time for a nice family lunch. This went on for years, and Mollie never objected. Jim would give her and the children a lift to church, where their sons sang in the choir, and she would meet neighbours for morning coffee in the church hall afterwards before strolling home.

When the children went off to college Mollie began to find Sunday mornings on her own a bit lonely. The only hint Jim got of this was her rather acid remark, 'I suppose you're off to the golf course again, are you?' one weekend. This aggressive comment not unnaturally put Jim on the defensive: 'Yes, I am. Got a problem with that?' Off he went, leaving Mollie feeling more cross with herself than she was with Jim. She would really have liked it if the two of them could have had the time together. But she was afraid that he wouldn't like it if she asked him straight out to change his golfing plans, and the only words she could find were sharp ones.

The atmosphere in their house on Sunday mornings got worse and worse. By now the accusation 'You never stay home on Sundays' had become part of Mollie's repertoire, and 'Not much point' had become part of Jim's. He now went off to play golf in such a foul mood that it spoiled his enjoyment of the game. He couldn't work out why his dear wife, usually so easy-going, had become so shrewish. He hadn't done anything different from what he'd been doing for years, after all.

When Jim got home one day, a full hour earlier than usual, he found Mollie staring out of the kitchen window with a cold cup of tea on the counter. He was taken aback by how sad she looked, and put his arms round her, saying, 'This is daft, lass. What's the matter with you?' And out came Mollie's tale of loneliness and woe, which Jim listened to with a mixture of relief and exasperation. He had been made to feel that he was in the wrong, when it seemed the truth was that Mollie really wanted to be with him. He was more than willing to spend his Sundays with her. Mollie had by this point realised that she did not want him to give up every Sunday, and a happy compromise was reached.

Instead of being able to say what she would like, Mollie could only speak of what she wasn't getting. Hearing only the accusation in her voice, Jim sprang to his own defence. If he had been aware of her sense of loneliness and loss, he would have been able to respond to it earlier. By not expressing her needs, Mollie began to weave a conversational pattern with Jim in which they both got the wires well and truly crossed.

Pause for thought

Have you got into a pattern of feeling disgruntled with your partner?

Is it because you regularly get your wires crossed when you want their attention?

Do you find yourself saying accusingly: 'You never listen to me' when what you really mean to say is: 'I need to talk to you'?

How often are you starting a sentence with the words 'You never . . .' when you're really trying to get attention?

In the next few days, try to listen to your own patterns of conversation with your partner. You might be surprised at what you hear, if you can be honest with yourself.

If you want to be listened to when you talk, there are some styles of speaking that you should try to avoid. The most obvious is the tendency to hold forth about whatever is on your mind regardless of the state of mind of the person listening. If you continually do this, the other person will eventually tend to switch off at the sound of your voice. It follows that when there is something serious you want to discuss you will have a hard time keeping their attention.

If there is something serious on your mind which you want to share, the most important rule is – say it. Choose a time when your partner can reasonably be expected to give you attention and when you will be free of interruptions, yes – but say it. This may seem obvious, but very often people shrink from coming out with what is really bothering them. One woman whose husband telephoned her first thing every morning when his work took him away from home was always brusque and said crossly that she didn't have time to talk. In fact she missed him dreadfully and wanted him to cut down on his travelling, but was afraid to say so. He felt rejected and increasingly resentful that the harder he worked the cooler she became.

__TELEPATHY GUARANTEES TROUBLE__

No matter how well you think another person knows you, no matter how close you feel to them or how long you have been together, never make the assumption that they can read your mind. Human beings cannot predict the future, and nor do they have the gift of clairvoyance when it comes to another person's thoughts and feelings.

It is very common for people to keep quiet about something that is bothering them or to say everything is all right when it is not. It is usually perfectly obvious from the aggrieved person's demeanour that something is wrong, even if nothing is being said or the problem denied. But the other person has no idea what the problem is – because in spite of asking, they haven't been told. They feel that the truth is being withheld from them, leaving them in a situation in which they feel they are being treated like a wrongdoer but given no opportunity either to plead their case or to put what is wrong right. They feel somehow responsible for their partner's discomfort.

People who refuse to say what they really mean cannot expect to get what they really want. This behaviour often occurs in families where silent disapproval is used to punish children guilty of minor transgressions. Children are disposed to want to please their parents and can suffer anguish when affection is denied them in this way. Adults who receive this sort of 'punishment' from their partners suffer too, but are much more likely to fight their corner, or even to get fed up and leave.

Owen and Pat had always used silence in their marriage as a kind of punishment. Whenever one of them felt put out by the other, a day of silence or minimal conversation would follow. Eventually they would make up and begin to speak. It was a familiar pattern to both of them and was how they had seen conflict being managed in their families of origin.

In the first few years of their relationship, making up often involved making love, and both would agree that they never wanted the sun to go down on their wrath. Gradually they let this promise slip and, more often than not, when they had words (they never had rows) and went to bed 'in a huff', they got up the next day still not speaking. Frequently, by the time they were back on speaking terms, they couldn't remember why they had taken umbrage in the first place.

By the time their sons left home this well-established 'silent treatment' was lasting for days and was seriously affecting their lives and had certainly killed off their sexual relationship. The effect on the family as a whole was that the children were reluctant to return home very often, for fear they would get caught up in an atmosphere of tense silence, because Pat would also mete out the silent treatment to her sons when they were growing up, and the more she did the more they felt sorry for their father.

Without their sons as go-betweens Owen and Pat found it less and less easy to break out of their cold-shoulder treatment of each other. During the period up to retirement, work made it possible to manage the difficult times in the marriage. In preparation for retirement, Owen – who was six years older than Pat – converted a small spare bedroom into an office with a radio transmitter. He was given a lot of the equipment by a new, recently widowed, neighbour whose husband had been a ham radio enthusiast. This new-found hobby drove Pat to distraction, for instead of Owen being 'sent to Coventry' by her silences she could hear him chatting happily away, unmoved by her refusal to speak to him.

The ham radio hobby came to an end after a few months, when Owen was told by council officials to take down his 30-foot aerial after complaints from neighbours. Pat was delighted. But Owen was not going to be deprived of his freedom from the 'treatment'. He simply installed a computer and learned how to surf the internet and use the e-mail. All Pat could hear now was the tapping of keys – and that was far worse.

In retirement, Pat watched television all day and Owen worked away at the computer. Eventually they ate their meals apart, slept apart, lived apart in the same house. The silence between them was deafening.

FIGHT OR FLIGHT

There are situations in which saying what you mean takes courage. But a minor problem left unsaid can grow into one that is much harder to resolve. Kept to yourself, a little niggle achieves disproportionate importance, not because it's a major issue in itself but because the effort of keeping it inside is using up huge amounts of your emotional energy.

There may be something your partner does which you would like done differently; you may be brooding over a health problem that you are frightened to face; there may be something worrying you about another member of the family or a problem at work that you cannot bring yourself to speak about. Resentment, anxiety and guilt can build up. You may think you are doing a good job of keeping it all to yourself, but these feelings seep out in sharp comments and distracted responses. Series of pointless rows erupt over trivial matters. Eventually one of you explodes and a major row ensues in which you both say things you later regret – and in which the original problem may not feature at all.

Internalising worries can affect your physical health as well as placing stress directly on your relationship. This can occur in later life in reaction to bereavement. Attempting to soldier on or to make a fresh start without giving yourself time to come to terms with loss is counter-productive. If you do not allow time for the loss and its meaning to be deeply felt, your body will show the signs of strain – in a range of symptoms from persistent headaches to irritable bowel syndrome and male erectile dysfunction.

Maria went to see a Relate counsellor because she thought her marriage was falling apart after more than thirty years. The problem was that Philip had simply stopped making love to her. Maria had contacted Relate in desperation. She felt very unhappy about making this move as she saw herself as someone who rarely had to seek help from anyone. She could count on the fingers of one hand the number of times she'd been to see a doctor in her life.

She was anxious to come on her own and it was the first thing she checked out when telephoning for the appointment. Although she had been reassured that this was fine, Maria arrived at the first meeting in an anxious state. She explained to her counsellor how uncomfortable she was talking about private things and how disloyal she felt in doing so. The counsellor, acknowledging how stressful such feelings were, invited Maria to tell her something of her story.

Philip and Maria had first met when he was stationed in Germany. She had gone to work as a civilian on the base a couple of months before Philip was due to return to the UK. It was love at first sight for both of them. When Philip was posted back to Yorkshire the romance continued with daily letters, and eventually Maria came to England for a holiday. They made that holiday a honeymoon, by marrying with a special licence.

By the time they were in their mid-thirties they had had two daughters and several postings, and they were tired of the demands of army life. Philip decided that they all needed a more settled life and took the first opportunity that came along to leave the Forces. He soon found a job using his fitter's skills on a car production line. They began what Maria called 'the best years'. They had weathered the normal ups and downs and trials and tribulations of married life. Their sex life had always been special since they first met, and although the years had seen a reduction in the frequency of love-making, it was still an important part of their lives. Until, that is, Philip 'gave up' on sex.

This had started about three years earlier when they were both fifty-eight and their youngest daughter had just got married. On a few occasions Philip had not been able to get his usual erection when they made love. At first Maria made little of this, putting it down to tiredness or one too many pints of beer. They both worked hard. Philip often worked overtime and didn't get home until eight.

She tried to talk to Philip about things, but he clearly didn't want to talk. He said talking wouldn't help, he'd be all right, he just had a lot on. Maria stopped making advances, feeling that would only put pressure on Philip and would not help the situation. Time passed. She noticed that Philip, who had always been an early-to-bed man, was watching more and more late-night television. When he did come to bed he went straight off to sleep. They had words about the lateness but not about the lack of sex.

Maria did not make a fuss when their love-making ceased altogether but privately felt more and more rejected. She hoped for improvement when they went on their annual holiday to Majorca but was disappointed. Philip, who always made the arrangements, had booked a twin-bedded room, explaining that it would be more comfortable in the heat.

Maria tried to make the best of it but she was at a loss to make sense of Philip's apparent acceptance of the situation. The more she thought about this the more unhappy she got. She began to fear that there might be another woman – that Philip might be having an affair and no longer loved her. He was an attractive man, and she had put on some weight since the menopause. She couldn't voice her fears and didn't dare to talk to her husband for fear of the answers she might have to face. It seemed like the only explanation, and yet it didn't really add up: Philip didn't spend much time away from home apart from going to work and supporting his favourite football team. She got herself in quite a state, became suspicious about everything and even thought about hiring a private detective.

It was at this point that Maria arrived at Relate. In talking to her counsellor she was helped to accept that the only way forward was to talk to Philip. It couldn't be put off. Together Maria and her counsellor rehearsed how, when and where would be the best time to begin. It took another session before Maria felt she understood more about their problem and felt confident enough to be able to open up the subject at home.

Maria did more than talk to Philip. She phoned to ask if it was all right to bring him to her next counselling session!

Philip had been amazed at what Maria told him. He had taken her no-fuss acceptance of the situation to mean that she didn't mind much and was happy not to be bothered. He had felt bad enough in himself about his lack of potency. The series of failures had shaken him. Using his own kind of logic, his strategy had been to avoid further failures and disappointments for Maria. He had remembered that his dad had hinted that he had had to 'shut up shop early in that department' and felt that history might be repeating itself. Philip had accepted what he thought was his fate, even though there were times when he felt sexual. He thought his erections were never firm enough to do anything with except occasionally masturbate.

During their joint counselling session, Philip and Maria resolved to do something about the situation. Philip was persuaded to see his GP to have a thorough medical check. The counsellor offered them reassurance and information. They learnt, for one thing, that the fact that Philip still got erections was a really positive sign. It was agreed that they would return after the appointment with the doctor.

Four weeks later when the counsellor saw them again they were all smiles. Philip had had a complete examination and some tests and had been given a clean bill of health. They both felt much better. They had agreed the previous week that they would go to bed at the same time 'just to cuddle'. They had been delighted when cuddling turned into their first sexual encounter for a long time. Maria was over the moon, as was Philip, though he was less confident. 'We mustn't think one swallow makes a summer, Maria,' he cautioned.

Over the next few weeks, continuing to see their counsellor, Philip and Maria rediscovered their lost sexual relationship. They came to see that their problem was not so much a sexual one but had rather more to do with the way they communicated with each other. They realised that in not talking about what was happening they had each misinterpreted the other's feelings and behaviour. They brought counselling to an end, determined to make up for lost time.

When we shrink back from facing the truth or speaking it, it is often because of fear: fear that we will be seen to be aggressive; fear that our request will seem ridiculous; fear that we will lose the other person's love and maybe even lose them. The paradox is that if you give in to the fear, as time passes these dreaded outcomes become more likely. If you can be honest about what's worrying you, nipping the problem in the bud so to speak, you might be a bit nervous when you speak, but it is far less likely that you will seem aggressive. You may even discover that, once out in the open, the problem actually is rather ridiculous, and see the funny side. (One woman was driven crazy last thing at night by the sound of her husband tapping his toothbrush on the side of the basin in the adjoining bathroom. She would lie there thinking murderous thoughts and turn over pointedly when he got into bed. When he finally managed to get her to say what was wrong they both fell out of bed laughing.)

You will probably find that, once you admit to worrying about something, your partner wants nothing more than to share your worries and help you to find a solution. That, far from being offended at being asked to change something or stop doing something, they will do their best to meet you half-way rather than upset you.

What is the alternative? What is the good of being able to say with a glow of virtue that you never get angry or raise your voice if you and your partner have never learned to tell each other the truth? Have you really kept your partner's love and respect if you have never showed them who you really are?

Those husbands and wives who sit together in restaurants, hardly speaking, could almost be strangers. Finding ways of bridging the silence takes effort and goodwill, that much is clear. But what are they going to talk about? This is not the time to deal with thorny issues or deep philosophical questions. And they know everything there is to know about each other already. Or do they? It's true that if you assume you know another person inside out, there is little point in asking for their views on what's in the news or going on in the neighbourhood. One of the first things you have to do, however, is test your own assumptions. Ask those questions with a real interest in the responses and you might get a surprise. And on the receiving end, take being asked for your opinions as a compliment. You might discover that you need to be better informed: if so, rejoice – these days, thanks to news on television and radio and in the newspapers, nothing could be easier.

NOBODY ELSE WILL

The writer Shirley Conran once said, 'Take a healthy interest in your own mind. If you don't, nobody else will.' Good advice. And the research also tells us that keeping mentally active makes a crucial contribution to the quality of life in the later years. We owe it to ourselves to make the most of the opportunities available to learn new skills or take part in new activities. Not only do they keep us fit and well in the widest sense, they also give us something to talk about. You can tell each other about the other people in your I.T. class or the silly story someone read out in your creative writing group. You can ask for ideas on what you could make in your carpentry class. You could see if your partner would like to take a holiday somewhere where you can put your new language to the test. You can talk about the countryside you saw on your last ramble and plan the next one. At this rate, your dinner will be getting cold.

There is a sense in which all transactions between partners are part of their sexual relationship with each other. All good conversations are a form of intimacy in themselves. Not only that, they are a necessary context for sexual intimacy. Women often say that making love starts long before they get into bed, in the words being exchanged between partners. Conversations in which couples really connect with each other are part of the ritual dance of relationships which are a preamble to the sexual 'dance'. Couples' capacity to have such conversations is vital: if you can't touch each others' hearts and minds, touching bodies can be empty gestures – actually a turn-*off*.

If you don't keep the lines of real communication open

between you, not only do you miss out on the full range of riches the relationship can offer, but when there is a problem (and sooner or later there will be, because life is changing all the time) you won't be equipped to deal with it. And if you don't deal with it adequately, the consequences are not that you will go on as you have always done (as if that was good enough) but there is the risk that the distance between you will get wider. Eventually this could lead to a disastrous break-up.

Mitch and Liz were a couple who paid a high emotional price for not being prepared to put some effort into talking to each other when they needed to. They had been married for thirty-six years when they came for counselling and had reached a point in their lives when they had time at their disposal. Neither of them worked any more and their children had long flown the nest to lead their own lives. They had established a routine which suited them both fairly well. Mitch had started to spend a lot of time in his greenhouse since retiring and become a bit of an expert on growing tomatoes. Liz had become involved in a series of coffee mornings and was often to be found chatting to a friend on the phone while Mitch was tending his plants. For many years it had been their custom to make love on Wednesday and Sunday nights. To be honest it had become a bit of a ritual.

Things changed when Liz had to have an operation on her bladder. When they eventually resumed love-making after her operation the pattern altered to once a week. And in fact it wasn't every week; their love-making became increasingly infrequent. Neither of them questioned what was happening (or rather, not happening) and neither attempted to discuss it. They just seemed to accept it. Mitch, knowing relatively little about the workings of the female anatomy, put it down to the operation. Liz had been the one to initiate sex for the first time after the operation and it had hurt a bit. This worried Mitch, and made him reluctant to make advances to Liz in future. He would wait for her to make the first move. Since she thought having a less active sex life was probably part of getting older, the occasions on which they made love grew fewer and fewer. Liz took to reading romantic novels, while Mitch watched the late film on TV.

Both Liz and Mitch still cared a lot for each other. They both missed the cuddles, the foreplay and the physical closeness that they had once enjoyed. But neither of them said a word until Mitch, who felt the loss most keenly, asked Liz if she would come with him to see a counsellor about the change that had taken place in their lives. Their earlier sex life may not have been passionate, but it had been a very important part of their marriage.

It was very hard for Mitch to put into words how he felt about what had happened. It wasn't as if he had come to see the counsellor because his marriage was terrible or because he was in deep despair. He certainly did not want anybody other than Liz. What came over was a kind of longing. Something that was important in his life was slipping away. He wanted to find out if it was natural to feel as he did, that he was being short-changed. He wanted to know if he had a right to try to retrieve what he and Liz had lost.

The counsellor encouraged Mitch and Liz to talk about what they expected from their sex life and from their life together in future. Somehow or other Liz's operation had become a kind of punctuation mark in their marriage: there was the life before, and the life after. It was almost a sign that now they were getting old. And both of them, but particularly Liz, were bedevilled by outdated ideas about how 'old' people should behave. Those ideas dictated that they should settle into a sleepy half-life, making no demands on themselves and resigning themselves to being dutiful, doting grandparents.

The counsellor challenged these assumptions with mention of people who, far from fading into the background at sixty, get a new burst of energy and attack life with gusto. But Liz couldn't shake off the image of what it was like to be sixty that she had unconsciously accepted. And although the months since the operation had left him a saddened man, Mitch could not find enough energy and commitment to stop the slide into a resigned acceptance that their love life was over. In their old routine, they'd never seen the need to think about whether they were really getting the best out of life – let alone talk about it. He had always gone along with what Liz wanted before, and he did so now.

Mitch and Liz let unspoken beliefs about how older people should behave stand in the way of their right to a measure of happiness. What was also very sad was that their ideas about sex were also so limited. They seemed to think that sex was only worth while if it culminated in penetration and inter-course. They couldn't get it into their heads that there was no reason why they couldn't continue to enjoy embracing, kissing, stroking, exploring and playing just as they had always done. None of these ways of giving and receiving love were forbid-den to them and all are potent sources of pleasure.

In the last session with the counsellor, Mitch came on his own. Part of him still hoped that he could find some means of connecting with Liz. But he was afraid of upsetting her. He was afraid that neither of them would be able to handle a con-versation about such an intimate part of their life. Old ideas and a lack of energy held him back from thinking in a new way. Thinking in a new way would have allowed him to behave in a new way; and that was his only hope of making a difference. They settled into a conventional old age. They start-ed to wear sensible, dull clothes. Their desultory conversations never went beyond the everyday, their communication limited, respectful and now emotionally distant. They hardly ever touched each other. And touch, as we shall see, is extraordinar-ily powerful.

Chapter Six

MEANING AND MISUNDERSTANDING

'Age cannot wither her': these were the words that Shakespeare wrote of Cleopatra, who was reputed to have enticed Antony away from his imperial duties. Using Shakespeare as our source of information, we know almost nothing about what Cleopatra looked like. But as time goes by, all bodies change. So unless she had been careful to avoid the North African sun, the chances are that the serpent of the old Nile had her fair share of wrinkles and that gravity had begun to have its inevitable effect on her looks. (Her powers of seduction were not affected.) The passage of time brings physical and biological changes to every human form. Because of their genetic make-up, some people experience these changes earlier than others. There is a huge variation, for example, in the age at which hair starts to turn grey (if at all) or become thinner.

Sensible people will take care of their physical health throughout their lives – not just to delay the onset of physical ageing or to minimise its effects. Eating a healthy diet, taking exercise, not smoking – these and other measures keep you fit and feeling good. It's not only practical, it is a sign of confidence in yourself to take care of your body.

In a society where youth and beauty are valued more highly than age and experience, there is a pressure to prove to the world that you still have value, not because of your advanced years but because 'you manage to stay so young' in spite of them. In a magazine interview the American film actress

Melanie Griffiths said that if she could have one wish it would be to have the body of a twenty-year-old attached to her forty-plus head, because then she 'wouldn't have to work out so hard to keep in shape'. Ms Griffiths is an exceptionally pretty woman with four lovely children, a handsome, successful husband and several homes. She has lived life to the full. And yet, in Hollywood, this is not enough. The danger is that this misconception will take hold closer to home.

If your response to the inevitable physical changes brought about by time is to try to fool yourself and everyone else that they are simply not happening, then you will indeed have to work very hard. It is more often women who fall for this trick, since it is they who have learned to equate sexual attractiveness with youth. Preserving the appearance of youth is time-consuming and can be expensive. And ultimately it doesn't work, because there is something profoundly unsexy about attempts to hold back the years. You cannot be sexy if you are not relaxed. And you cannot be relaxed if you are over-anxious about your appearance. The ancient Romans had an expression – *noli me tangere*, roughly translated as 'hands off' – which neatly sums up the unspoken message given out by a woman whose hair is lacquered into submission. Nor is anyone who spends so much time and attention on themselves likely to be a generous-spirited companion.

Men who are anxious about their fading youth might try equally hard to look young, with unseasonal tans and carefully concealed bald spots. But where virility has been thought so vital, the trappings of continuing power take on a new importance. Hence the flashy sports car or the significantly expensive watch that tells the time in five continents. The continuing need to exercise power may show itself in pursuing hobbies and activities not for their intrinsic pleasure, but simply to win prizes for the fastest lap or the biggest catch. Sometimes the new, young girlfriend is used as an outward symbol of continuing virility. Sadly, someone who is so concerned to convince the world of his stature is unlikely to be a considerate lover.

The third age – the years past fifty – will for many last for around thirty years. Having entered it, you will continue to change. There is no real alternative but to accept it. You can choose to shrug off the youth and beauty mantra and relax into being the person your fairly long and interesting life has made you. You cannot make the most of this wonderful gift of time if you pretend it isn't happening. Many older couples cite a relaxed acceptance of each other as they are as one of life's joys. From this flows the freedom to express your sexuality and to explore its meaning in your life.

THE MEANING OF SEX

Ageism in matters sexual misses the point. An assumption that good sex should be measured by performance – how often, for how long (back to numbers again) or how athletic – disregards what makes a sexual relationship enriching and enduringly pleasurable. Many older people who have enjoyed a long and rewarding sexual relationship with their partner would say that it is often not until they reached their mature years that they began to understand the meaning of sex. It is tempting to think that sex might even be wasted on the young.

Reaching this understanding might happen slowly. Or it might be arrived at unexpectedly. This is how it was for Hughie, who after sixteen years of his second marriage brought his wife Sarah with him to see a counsellor. For most of those years he had, in his own words, 'put up with' not being allowed enough sex. It made him resentful; he had an almost permanent feeling of being just fed up with everything – and Sarah did not look any more cheerful.

Hughie was glad that they were seeing a male therapist, James. He felt sure that another man would understand that it was absolutely natural for him to want more sex. And James did agree that Hughie had a perfect right to want more sex. He also said that he thought Sarah had a perfect right to want less. James thought that the question they ought to be looking at was what Hughie wanted sex for.

Exasperated by what he saw as a stupid question, Hughie reminded James that every man had his needs, by which he meant the desire for sexual excitement and the release of orgasm. James reminded Hughie that if that was what he wanted he could allow it to himself every day by masturbating. The level of exasperation increased at this point, as Hughie found he had to explain what was missing from this practical solution. 'It's obvious,' he said to James. 'There's no one there wanting you.' James finally got him to spell it out: what Hughie had really meant when he said he wanted more sex – and what he thought he had been saying all along – was that he wanted to feel wanted and desired. At the sound of these words Sarah, who until this point had sat silent and subdued, raised her eyes to look at her husband.

It was at a later session that Sarah gave voice to her own thoughts about sex. She didn't really understand why men thought it was so important, but she did believe that Hughie's desire to possess her sexually was a sign of his regard. It showed that he had noticed her and that he liked what he saw. Her experience of sexual intercourse was that it seemed to be more fulfilling for Hughie than it was for her, although sometimes she climaxed and enjoyed it. What really mattered was that he should be loving towards her. The more loving and attentive he was out of bed, the more responsive she found herself being when they were in bed.

By the time Hughie and Sarah came to see James, each was blaming the other for what was wrong with their sexual relationship. As they talked and listened to each other, it became clear that they both wanted the same thing – to feel loved and desired. Sex was the ultimate way of giving and receiving what they both wanted. But because sex had acquired different meanings for them both, the transaction kept going wrong more often than it went right.

During the war, Hughie had been involved in mine clearance. 'A heart in mouth job' was how he described the delicate and dangerous work he had been called upon to do – 'one false move and you're done for'. Sexual encounters with Sarah had become like that, he said: he would approach her with tremendous care, and not much confidence, fearing the worst. The worst outcome was to be rejected. His fear was that his precious gift, his sexuality, would be spurned. But for all that, Hughie was not one to give up, and he would keep trying to get (and give) what he wanted. The trouble was, all Hughie's attempts to reach his goal made the problem worse for Sarah.

Over the years of being a wife and mother, Sarah had felt increasingly less important as a person and less interesting to Hughie. A certain degree of boredom set in, and sex became just one of the many duties she had to carry out. At their best times in the early days, sex had been what she lovingly gave to her partner, much of her pleasure deriving from his obvious delight. As the years went by, however, it was yet another task she felt obliged to perform before the end of the day. Even plucky Hughie's enthusiasm for the task began to fade. On one occasion Hughie actually stopped moving inside Sarah, and she remained unresponsive. He was hurt and angry; she was hurt and confused. It was this unhappy event that prompted them to seek help.

Sex had acquired a whole range of different meanings for Hughie and Sarah during their marriage. For him it had always been a desirable prize, always before him but tantalisingly out of reach. It was a commodity which his wife rationed out, making it a challenge to please her so that she would increase the ration. It had come to mean as likely as not a rebuff. Sex had now come to represent an anxious experience which did little for his self-esteem.

Set next to this Sarah's set of meanings. Sarah found sex rather mysterious, and yet felt she had to manage it somehow or it would get out of hand. For her it had always been a precious gift that she could bestow as a token of love. From a pleasant enough experience for her personally, it then became a burdensome duty. Sex had now come to represent an experience in which it was obvious she was a disappointment to her partner.

Hughie and Sarah came to understand that their different 'meanings' for sex had led them to misunderstand each other and each other's needs. In working with their counsellor, they came to a realisation that their different meanings were not irreconcilable. Each could have their needs met, now that understanding was a possibility.

SEXUAL SIGNALS

There is always a signalling system in operation between couples – a telepathic communication pattern – a code indicating interest in or readiness for sex. A woman might say, for example, 'I think I'll have an early bath tonight.' A man might turn to his wife as she sits next to him on the sofa looking at the television and ask, 'Are you watching this?' What both are really saying is, 'I feel like making love. I want to make love with you. Please come to bed with me.'

Sometimes the signal is a touch, rather than spoken: it might be subtle and gentle or obviously lustful. To start with, the predictability of the signalling system is comforting. You both know where you are. As time goes by, routines get established. Routine itself can, however, have a deadening effect the longer it continues. For a lot of people, the signalling system that once worked every time gets stale. The partner receiving the signal begins to feel taken for granted. What once had a flavour of excitement becomes mechanical – like pressing button B in the old telephone boxes to get your money back.

Take a man who always splashed on a certain cologne when he wanted to have sex with his wife. When the full extent of his courtship is a splash of old favourite and he expects her to be turned on, all that happens is that her heart sinks. With no kisses, no caresses, no soft words, his signal is having exactly the opposite effect.

Ernest always used to stroke the back of his wife Heather's neck in a particular way when he wanted to start making love. For no reason that he could work out, she began to wriggle away from him and then to give him a withering glance every time he did this, so that now he hardly dares to make a move.

When Paddy got home from work in the middle of the afternoon, his wife Deb would inevitably be at the sink washing up, and he would sidle up to her and put his hands up her skirt and say, 'Are we on, then?' For ages the kitchen was the scene of their most passionate embraces – and then Deb began to push him away. Paddy was mortified.

In all these situations a failure to update the language and renegotiate the situation led to trouble. Relationships that have endured for years last because each partner strikes a balance between the comfort of the familiar and the stagnation of the predictable. As well as making an effort to keep their contact fresh and not taking the other for granted, each learns to understand the slightly different signalling systems used by the opposite sex. The signals are different because the settings in which men and women feel sexy are slightly different. Women need more time, and will take steps to ensure that they get it. When a woman snuggles up to her man on the sofa and starts nuzzling his neck, she is trying to create the romantic setting which will enable her to move on to feeling aroused. If her dearly beloved is watching the rugby, the chances are that she will not succeed. There are many reasons why what works on one occasion fails to do so on another: signalling systems can be contrary and unpredictable, too.

Men have the ability to be aroused more immediately upon contact. But in later life, men too need more time to become aroused, and the opportunity is there for both partners to synchronise their moves. Both must take responsibility for this. Deb, predictably at the sink, needed to change her pattern too if she wanted to set a different tone for the language of love with her partner. Paddy's approach and chat-up line clearly needed updating! Heather needed to let Ernest know that the time had come for a new way of initiating sex. Continuing to operate the telepathic signalling system had to stop and be renegotiated.

Chapter Seven

BREAKING THE MOULD

Helen is in her early forties. She runs a small business from home, her husband having gone back to college for a year to acquire a new qualification in his field. Christmas is a busy time of year for her and when her sister rang up one day, she wasn't able to talk for long. 'I'm exhausted,' she said. 'We were invited out on Saturday night by someone Richard's met in his seminar group. They didn't serve the meal until ten and we didn't get away until half past two. We just can't take the pace any more!'

As they talked it became clear that confusion about what constitutes bedtime was not simply down to lack of stamina on the part of Helen and her husband. Because Richard's field is software development – a relatively young business – most of his colleagues and fellow-students are relatively young, too: happy to stay up half the night listening to music, chatting about nothing in particular and sleeping through most of Sunday. You could say it's a lifestyle choice; but it's not a choice open to Helen and Richard, one of them with a backlog of orders to meet on Monday morning and the other keen to get back on the career ladder several rungs higher than when he left it. At this stage, their priorities are focused on achieving security, forging ahead in the career stakes and consolidating their home.

Like many people of their generation, Helen and Richard are planning to retire in their mid-fifties; or if not that, at least to reduce their work commitments by half, scaling down to nothing, or very little, by sixty. More and more people are seizing the opportunity offered by flexible working patterns and continued good health to construct a new and full life when their working years are over. A number of things make such plans possible: financial and domestic security, successfully launching a family, satisfaction with a job well done so far as a career is concerned. More than that, your status is no longer defined solely by the answer to the question: 'And what do you do?' Those who have already reached their fifties and sixties are blazing a trail as they learn to exploit new possibilities.

With the advent of retirement, you enter a new period of freedom: freedom from the nine-to-five grind; freedom from striving to achieve promotion; freedom from the constriction of roles somebody else has set for you; freedom to pursue some of the things you've only dreamed about before; freedom to be yourself and to enjoy life together. The only factors that might limit what you do are restricted funds and less than perfect health; but when it comes to ideas about what 'older people' should and shouldn't do – they belong on the scrapheap. Research conducted at the department of old-age psychology at the University of Edinburgh by Dr David Weeks has pinpointed the factors that empower people to feel young – in other words, to enjoy a high quality of life. Sociability, curiosity, enthusiasm and optimism are the qualities that make the difference.

The truth is that even if you feel lacking in these gifts, they can be cultivated. It is a virtuous circle: interacting with people and keeping your brain active is fun; once you start, it's hard to stop. In 1999, some 7,000 people over the age of sixty enrolled on courses offered by the Open University. They signed up to study subjects as varied as science, art history and modern languages. If you want to learn a new language or brush up your schoolbook French, you can go to daytime or evening classes. There are hundreds of courses in the UK accredited by the Open College Network. The Workers' Educational Association (WEA) offers courses on everything from historic buildings to computing skills. Since it was set up in 1982, The University of the Third Age has formed 400 groups with 87,000 members around the country. These groups exist to provide daytime education and leisure activities for retired men and women at minimal cost. They draw upon the knowledge, experience and skills of their members to organise study groups which offer more than 300 subjects in areas such as art, foreign languages, poetry and theatre-going. Look on the noticeboard in your local library: typically, the choice of activities on offer is staggering, whether you want to be a warden at the nature reserve, learn ballroom dancing, join the writing guild or take a student under your wing in the adult literacy scheme. Growing older is no reason not to try new activities. Mary Wesley was seventy when she wrote her first novel, *Jumping the Queue*, since when she has become a much-loved writer. A novelist of an earlier era, Leo Tolstoy, was sixty-seven when he learned to ride a bike. Popeye waited until he was seventy to ask for Olive Oyl's hand in marriage!

Pause for thought

Are there things you've always wanted to do and never have?

Is it a long list? If it is, ask yourself, 'What am I waiting for?'

Ask yourself what is really stopping you.

What is getting in the way and what can you do about it?

What would be first on the list of things to learn?

What do you need to do to get started? Ask at the library?

Check out the local evening classes? Ring up a college?

As well as numberless opportunities for personal development, the third age brings with it the chance to take personal relationships into a new phase. Learning to appreciate it is an interesting process in itself. Those who were teenagers in the 1960s had an image of what their mums and dads and aunts and uncles were like at fifty or sixty. They seemed to be a bit creaky, a bit tired and a bit dull. Here you now are, more than fit enough to blow out sixty candles on your birthday cake, and finding it necessary to rewrite the script. Being given a clean sheet of paper is exciting, but it is also somewhat daunting. If you are not Darby and Joan, and don't want to be Tarzan and Jane, who are you?

————————— NEW BEGINNINGS ————————

Working out where you belong in the new scheme of things in later life is a question that might be asked as keenly by men and women who find new partners as by couples who have been together for a period of years. Like Gerald, who, at sixty-four, had been divorced for ten years. His ex-wife had remarried and emigrated to New Zealand, but his married daughter Claire lived just down the road with her family. She called in each evening after he came home from work, bringing him dinner, sorting out his laundry, getting things he needed when she did the weekly shop.

The routine of Gerald's life was pleasantly interrupted when he met Elaine at a mutual friend's wedding anniversary party. Like himself, Elaine, aged fifty-six, was divorced. They started to go out together – having lunch in a country pub he liked, going to listen to concerts by the local brass band; some Saturday nights they went to see a film. Claire didn't seem too pleased by this turn of events. When Gerald told her about his new friendship all she could say was: 'You want to be sure she's not after your money, Dad.' Gerald found himself on the defensive: he had come to like Elaine more and more in the few months they had been going out together and begun to realise how much he had missed having someone special to share things with. They began to stay over at each other's houses at weekends. They became lovers, and life was good.

It didn't last. Claire reacted badly to the fact of her father's obvious sexual involvement with Elaine. She said she was 'embarrassed' to see his bedroom light go on so early in the evening – claimed his grandchildren were 'shocked' by his behaviour – declared that her husband was 'sickened' to see his father-in-law involved with 'mutton dressed as lamb'. She didn't pull her punches, and Gerald was deeply upset. These harsh words were hurtful to hear, and their effect was to begin to chip away at Gerald's confidence. His relationship with Elaine had become very important to him but, stung by his daughter's criticisms, he found himself wondering whether he should end it – the next minute feeling hopeless at the thought of losing her.

As this state of confusion continued, Gerald became less and less able to respond sexually, losing his erections half-way through love-making. For her part, Elaine was patient and simply accepted that this was happening without making a fuss. But Gerald was privately devastated. He found himself feeling tense all the time and easily irritated. Concerned that there might be a physical cause, Gerald consulted his doctor. After medical examinations made it clear that nothing organic was wrong, the doctor asked Gerald if there were any sources of pressure or tension in his life – and the simmering resentment from his daughter came to mind.

The doctor suggested to Gerald that he might find it helpful to talk to the Relate counsellor attached to the health practice. In the discussions that followed, Gerald explained that his daughter's critical words had made him 'feel ashamed and dirty'. It had seemed to him, after Claire's outburst, as if he had no right to a love life – a potentially rewarding life which he was deeply reluctant to give up. Gerald went to see the counsellor three times in as many months. During their sessions, he came to realise that his daughter was placing expectations on him that, if fulfilled, would deny him what he both needed and deserved: the rewards of love and intimacy. He saw that he and Elaine had a right to express their affection and desire for each other without disapproval. He was determined to claim that right.

Mixed in with a sense of relief and a celebratory renewal of his love-making with Elaine, was a regretful pity for Claire. Gerald came to see that she had become fixed in attitudes about sex, attitudes which had threatened his happiness in the present but which, if she were not able to examine them, would eventually threaten her own. He asked Elaine what she thought they could do to help Claire. Elaine said she thought the best thing was to set a good example – and have an early night.

Pause for thought

Gerald was badly affected by his daughter's disapproving attitude.

Do you worry too much about how others see you?

Does it restrict what you want to do with your life and who you see?

Would you really lose your place with them if you behaved differently after all these years?

STARTING AGAIN

There are countless people of fifty or sixty-plus who are looking for or finding a new relationship. It may be because their first partner has died or because they have divorced after years of marriage. Increasing numbers of men and women have never married because they have had very demanding careers. Some, like Marian, may not have married because they have devoted years to caring for an elderly relative who has now died. Many women have brought their children up alone and, when the children are grown, want to make a new adult relationship. Each of these situations is different.

Take Frances, for example. She was fifty-two when she and her husband divorced. At that point she took on a full-time secretarial job at the health practice where she had been working three days a week ever since their son started primary school. He had just got a place at art college and Frances needed to boost her earnings. And she enjoyed working in the busy practice with people coming and going all day long. She liked all her workmates, too, and stayed there right up to her retirement, aged sixty. Until that day she had always had the excuse of being too busy to spend more time with Trevor, a widower she had met the summer before on a coach tour of the Italian Lakes. Now there was no convincing reason for refusing his invitations to come and spend the weekend with him. It wasn't that she didn't like him: they had really hit it off on the holiday and (both great letter-writers) had kept it touch in the intervening six months, occasionally meeting up for a day out. The real reason for her refusal was that Frances felt confused and awkward about embarking on a sexual relationship after such a long time. Neither of the two relationships she had had since her divorce had come to that point, but she had a feeling that it would be different with Trevor.

Her mind was in a spin. What were Trevor's expectations of a weekend together? Would the friendship collapse if she did go but then refused to sleep with him? She wasn't ready for that, but did want to go on seeing her new friend and get closer to him. How far should they go? Would it all be horribly embarrassing? How long could she put off replying to his invitation? Would it be better to call the whole thing off?

Frances did what lots of us do in similar situations and threw herself into useful displacement activity – in her case, taking cuttings from overwintered geraniums. Luckily she was interrupted by a visit from Maggie, one of the community nurses from her old practice out on her rounds, hoping for a cup of coffee with her old friend. Maggie could tell that Frances was a bit agitated, and it didn't take long for her to spill the beans to someone she trusted.

Next to them on the sideboard were all the retirement cards well-wishers had sent to Frances. Looking at them, she said she felt more like an inexperienced sixteen-year-old than a retired lady. Chatting to Maggie, Frances began to see that the situation had a funny side as they talked through all the possible scenarios, including trying to think through how Trevor himself might be feeling.

Frances's sense of confusion, retired lady as she was, had a lot to do with the myths about men and women she and many others of her generation were handed when she really was sixteen. How many women of her age remember the immortal words 'Give them an inch and they'll take a mile'? Behind those words of warning to innocent virgins is a clutch of misguided notions: that if a man gets an erection while he's in your company, it's your doing and you've got to do something about it. That the very sight of your knees (or ankles, or modest

---

Pause for thought

Below are six commonly held beliefs about men and women and sexual behaviour – ideas that we grow up with and may have outgrown. Some myths persist, however. Consider for a moment if you have believed them in the past and whether they still ricochet around in your thinking in the present.

Men find it difficult to control themselves once aroused.
Getting a man excited without going on to have sex is unfair.
Women prefer large penises.
To have sex a man must have an erection.
Women don't feel sexual after the menopause.
Women can't enjoy sex if they don't have a climax.

cleavage) is likely to inflame him to such a pitch that he cannot control himself (so you have to). But such ideas do a disservice to males and females alike, painting men as pathetic creatures who cannot control their urges and women as cold-blooded incapable of any sexual feelings of their own.

Hand in hand with the sexual myths are the social taboos that for many a long year restrained women from taking any initiative in relationships. Under cover of the requirement to be 'a nice girl', women brought up before the 1960s learnt to wait: wait to be asked out, wait to be asked to dance, wait to speak, wait to be told what to do and even to think. For women like Frances, and there are very many like her, these injunctions do not prove very useful in the real world.

At a later stage in the book, in Chapter Thirteen, there is a further opportunity to think about current myths about sex and older people.

What does all this mean in the context of Frances's indecision about Trevor? First and foremost, that Frances had just as much right to dictate the pace of their developing friendship as he did. As Maggie pointed out, they met as equals: two adults who had bought themselves holidays and decided for themselves how they wanted to spend their time off. They saw each other as equals: coming to amicable agreement about whether to go on that day's excursion or to stay by the lakeside, for example; whether to have dinner in the hotel or find a trattoria in the town. As Frances's equal, in maturity, experience, and sensitivity – as he seemed to be – Trevor was more than capable of hearing that yes, she would like to spend a weekend with him but thinks she ought to make it clear that she isn't ready for anything but a developing friendship at this point. Frances was aware that it was not particularly flattering to Trevor to imagine that he would not respect her wishes. And in fact he would be just as likely as she to be apprehensive of a seduction scene. Probably all he wanted was a nice weekend together as well.

It is salutary to remember that no one ever actually died of embarrassment. There is no shortage of opportunities in life for little blips, especially at close quarters, that might cause a stutter (the clash of colliding spectacles as you embrace is one you can count on). Little blips prove that you're both human, which makes you that much more loveable. The situation is retrievable (next time remove the spectacles first) and no harm is done by losing a tiny bit of dignity for a moment. Take Louella, who, having 'lost her dignity' on a Caribbean holiday, returned determined to do something about it.

Louella came to England with her family just after the war. She was ten. Her family were hard-working. Her father worked on the London Underground and her mother was a hospital ward orderly. Louella worked hard at school and like the rest of her family attended an Evangelist church regularly every Sunday, singing in the youth choir. When she was sixteen, she delighted her family by getting a place as a trainee nurse.

Louella was a dedicated nurse and loved her job. She qualified as a midwife and by the time she was thirty-five she had become sister on a large obstetrics and gynaecological ward. Her life was divided between work and church. Years passed. Louella never married, saying laughingly that she never had the time and that anyway she had never met anyone who took her fancy. On her mother's death, she became a support for her father and surrogate mother to her brothers and sisters. She was seen as the unadventurous, dutiful daughter, sister and aunt by her nephews and nieces. She'd always promised her favourite niece that one day, when she had retired, she would take her to St Lucia so that she could know where the family came from.

When they finally made the trip, a two-week package deal, the unexpected happened. Louella fell in love. Winston was a very distant relative whom she met at a welcome party thrown by her St Lucia cousins. In the way of the Caribbean, it was a very boisterous and lively occasion. Winston made Louella feel attractive in a way she had not felt for years. At first, she didn't trust his attentions, but as the days went on it seemed that Winston was more and more serious in his intentions. Louella felt like a teenager. When she was with Winston, they laughed and joked a lot. And although the holiday only lasted two weeks, by the end of it the pair of them were inseparable. There was only one blot on an otherwise clear horizon. Winston wanted sex. And Louella was still a virgin at sixty-two. Her obstetrics and gynaecology experience meant that she wasn't exactly ignorant of the subject but she had never had more than a heavy petting relationship in the past – and that was decades earlier. When she hadn't let her earlier boyfriend 'have his way', determined to save herself for marriage, he had left her in the lurch. On one occasion Winston tried to make love to Louella, but without success. The relationship remained unconsummated and Louella returned to England still a virgin.

She invited Winston to come to the UK and promised that she would return to St Lucia on a regular basis. Once home, she expected to hear nothing more from Winston and was surprised at how regularly he wrote and phoned. He couldn't afford to come to England so Louella decided to go back to see him six months later.

Louella knew that she really needed to do something about the sex. Less troubled now by religious restrictions, she sought out the help of a Relate sex therapist. Louella worried that at sixty-two, she would be unable to have a sexual relationship at all. She wanted to find a way of proving that she could. As a nurse, she had seen operations where young women with a condition called vaginismus (a spasm of the vagina) had their vaginas stretched under anaesthetic. This certainly didn't appeal to her and she couldn't envisage herself asking her GP to refer her for treatment. She wasn't even sure that she did have the condition.

With the help of the therapist, Louella was able to do exercises with graded dilators which she inserted into her vagina, initially when she was in the bath and later when she was lying down on her bed. The dilators were graded in size and specially made for the job. The first size was the size of a little finger and the final size was the size of an average penis. It was to Louella's credit that she persevered with the exercises even though at times in her anxiety she found the task of inserting the dilators embarrassing and difficult. In six weeks, Louella gained the confidence that she could indeed have sex and that she could return to St Lucia to test-drive this new-found confidence. Winston proved to be a patient lover and Louella a willing pupil. Her family were delighted when they announced that they would marry and Louella would return to her place of birth to live with Winston. Now, every year, she is visited by nieces and nephews who never thought to have a married aunt, let alone a new uncle.

NEW PATTERNS

Sometimes you have to take a bit of a risk and show a little faith, as when circumstances change the pattern of long-standing friendships. Juliette had been friends with Mary for years, ever since as young mothers they met at the school gate and found out they were almost neighbours. Their children had been in and out of each other's houses and both families had become close – Juliette's husband Dan liked to take all the boys to watch rugby; Mary's husband Connor taught all the children to swim. They had wonderful holidays camping in Devon. When the children had left home and the two men had retired, the two couples planned a long series of weekend treats for themselves, working their way through all the cathedral cities. About every four months they'd be off to York or Gloucester or Canterbury, always finding a comfortable family hotel and searching out a nice country pub for Sunday lunch. It was a terrible shock to them all when Juliette had a fatal heart attack at the age of sixty-six.

At first Mary and Connor didn't think Dan would want to

go with them when, six months later, they suggested a visit to Durham. But he did go, and the continuing friendship was a support to the three of them. Then, about two and a half years later, Connor died. Mary was now sixty-eight, and Dan seventy-three – old friends with a shared history, close to each other's children, fond of each other's grandchildren. They were comfortable together.

Mary felt it as a threat to that sense of comfort when, shortly after the first Christmas she had spent as a widow, Dan asked her to marry him. She simply hadn't seen it coming and could only stammer a reply to the effect that she would have to think about it. Which, when she did think about it on her own afterwards, struck her as inadequate and possibly even rude. She thought about it a lot, and tried to work out what had made her feel so confused and how she could sort out the tangle. She realised that it must have taken a great deal of courage for Dan to ask the question; she recognised that they were both lonely now that their lifetime partners had gone; but she knew that while she placed enormous value on Dan's friendship, and did not want to lose it, a friend was what she wanted, not a lover and not a husband.

This was what Mary had to find a way of telling Dan. He had taken the risk; she had to have faith in the bond of their long friendship and be truthful with him. She chose her moment carefully and put it as gently as she could. He was disappointed, although he pretended not to be. And for a while afterwards, it was a bit awkward, and things were slightly strained between them. In time they recovered their old easy ways together, but both of them had consciously to work at valuing what they had as friends when it might have been tempting to withdraw in disappointment.

One of the thoughts in Mary's head was that, paradoxically enough, although she and Dan knew each other so well, there was much they didn't know. The joys of her marriage to Connor, and it had been a good marriage, were part of a private world that she kept to herself. She chose not to start a new voyage of discovery with a new partner. For her, a peaceful friendship was more than enough.

Not everyone who has been widowed feels the same way. Dan was one of those who, after the shock and sadness of loss and the turmoil of mourning, reached a point where part of carrying on living meant trying to form a new relationship.

BEEN THERE, DONE THAT

Some elements of forming a new relationship never change; others do. When you form a new relationship in later life, for example, the fact that you have an older head on your shoulders makes a difference. When you are young, you're test-driving bits of your life all the time – you think you know what you want but keep having to try it out.

Older people have already done an awful lot of that trying out. Having travelled a long way down the road, you have a sense of what you want. This applies to quite trivial things as well as more important ones. Young men have a go at all sorts of hobbies before they find one they really like, and by that time there's a guitar, a set of golf clubs and a complicated camera gathering dust. The bathroom shelf of a younger woman is often crowded with six or seven different kinds of shampoo and there might be about the same number of lipsticks in her handbag; a more mature woman will have worked out which one she needs. What doesn't change is the need to continually negotiate and renegotiate your relationships, if they are to remain alive and kicking and if you are not to feel taken for granted.

When you are young and first married or setting out on the major relationship of your life, both partners still have a degree of flexibility about male and female roles. Leaving aside for a moment commonly held notions of what 'a woman's place' is or what it means 'to be a real man', at the domestic level there is always room for variation. At the beginning of a relationship

---

Pause for thought

Do you know what you like or do you only know what you don't like?

It's fairly simple to allow yourself to like chocolate and hate sprouts – but what about the likes and dislikes in relationships?

How did you find out what you like in a partner?

Trial and error?

Bitter experience?

How did you decide what was important and what not?

---

forged in your young years, finding your feet as husband and wife is part of the adventure. Neither of you is really that certain about the right way or the best way to do things, but you're prepared to try things out and, confident of your love for each other, to be forgiving when they don't always work out. And if you cannot always be forgiving at first, a sense of humour can often save the day.

Apparently insignificant rituals can illustrate the point. Celia was all set to go home to mother only two weeks after getting married because she couldn't persuade her new husband, Jack – who always helped with the washing up – to give the dishcloth a good wringing out afterwards and drape it over the taps to air. (His way was to give it a limp squeeze and leave it on the draining board.) The farcical nature of the situation came home to her when she stood in the hall with her coat on and realised that actually she couldn't go anywhere unless Jack took her on the back of his motorbike. It was an early lesson in the need to negotiate and also to acknowledge that you can both be right.

Chapter Eight

HEALTHY NEGOTIATION AND RENEGOTIATION

After twenty or more years of marriage, couples naturally evolve their own 'truths' about their respective roles and expectations, from little day-to-day matters to weightier issues. Sorting them out is part of getting to know each other, and can mean having to face questions you'd never really thought about before. 'Sorting them out' is perhaps a misleading expression, implying that things actually do get sorted out once and for all, when in fact the process is never-ending. Having satisfactorily dealt with the dishcloth problem, Jack and Celia are now working on the big question of whether to iron freshly washed clothes before putting them in the suitcase or waiting until arrival at their holiday destination, when the clothes will be creased anyway.

What happens as a result of constantly being willing to engage in the process is that you get better at it: you evolve a style of negotiating that works for you. By definition, negotiation requires flexibility and a willingness to listen as well as being able to put your own ideas into words. The styles that work best are those developed by couples who recognise that they can both be right, who are able to acknowledge when they are not, to be forgiving of each other and to laugh with each other.

Negotiation in a marriage or long-term relationship is a never-ending process. It is what happens when you share information, when you say how you feel, telling it how it is. And also hearing how it is, learning about what is felt by your partner. The word 'negotiation' has become associated with all manner of business and commercial activities, but in reality we all do it every day. Putting the question 'Shall we go to Tesco's?' and dealing with the response is a simple negotiation. There are countless everyday situations in which you are, whether you are aware of it or not, constantly negotiating – in a relationship with someone – particularly if you are living with them, in a workplace setting, booking a holiday, choosing vegetables from the market stall. All the transactions of your daily life have an element of negotiation – it is not a word you need to fear. Don't think you have to be Henry Kissinger to do it. It is something you started to learn how to do even when you were very small and persuaded your mum to buy you a Mars bar or let you stay up late enough to watch *Sunday Night at the London Palladium*.

The effectiveness of a style of negotiating can often be measured in the context of a new situation – and entering a new phase in a long-term relationship offers just that opportunity. David and Kay, whose story we looked at on page 10 discovered that they had to develop a completely new way of communicating with each other in order to make the most of their future together. Martin and Carol, on the other hand, to all intents and purposes side-stepped the issue, as one partner established what he believed to be the right way and the other complied with it.

Malcolm and Janet had been married for thirty-six years when they both took planned early retirement. They had worked hard all their lives, Malcolm as an accountant with a large firm, Janet as senior administrator in the local teaching hospital. They had brought up a son who now lived in Canada with his wife and three children. Throughout their lives Janet and Malcolm had successfully avoided any friction or conflict by having a lot of interests which took them out of the home. Both were involved in local politics, she as a parish councillor, he as a borough councillor. When they weren't at work or meetings there were always people at their front door wanting help with this dispute or that planning issue.

The truth was that Janet and Malcolm had found a very satisfactory way of managing their lives in a way that limited the intimacy between them. Early on in their marriage both had recognised, although neither had ever put it into words, that their 'grand passion' had petered out because they felt suffocated by too much closeness. They established lives that meant they didn't have to face this issue. Their sexual relationship became infrequent – limited to holidays and anniversaries. Life was too busy for sex. Eventually when either of them commented on how little time they had to do things together they comforted themselves with thoughts of setting things right when they retired.

But retirement brought them unexpected problems, for each had a different view of what it would mean. Malcolm was looking forward to having more time for himself, and Janet was looking forward to having more time to do things together. Each assumed the other understood their point of view and each got more and more frustrated as they tried to establish a new pattern of life. They had always been proud of the fact that they didn't row but now they bickered and sniped at each other constantly.

After a year they were seriously considering separating, with Janet convinced that Malcolm had undergone some serious personality change. What neither of them had recognised was that in having very busy lives, they had not really needed to negotiate closeness and distance.

Some serious renegotiation was due and it happened while they were on holiday with their closest friends. Trouble had been brewing for most of the day with the two of them openly critical of each other. By the time dinner was over their friends had had enough and threatened to return home if Malcolm and Janet didn't sort themselves out. Embarrassment forced them to put their cards on the table and unravel their differing views and disappointments. Malcolm had felt that Janet's need for 'doing things together' would take over his time for himself and smother him. Janet saw Malcolm's reluctance to do things together as a selfish rejection of her needs. For the first time they acknowledged their disappointment in their sexual relationship. Over the next few days they were very careful with each other, checking and re-checking what was said and trying to make sure that their wires didn't get crossed.

When they got home they had one or two bad days. The big difference was that having recognised the need to change and to avoid making assumptions it became much easier to agree about both what they did as a couple and what they did independently.

When two people form a new relationship in later life, they each bring to it a history. Falling in love at sixty may well make you feel sixteen again – it may even make you *behave* as if you were sixteen again, too, and good luck to you – but the experience of the years is there. Each partner is likely to have been married before or to have been in a long-term relationship before, during which 'truths' about what it means to be a husband or a wife have been built up. You may continue, at an unconscious level, to hold these 'truths'; you may, on the other hand, be determined to shed them. As you start to form a new intimate friendship you will encounter both your own and your new partner's ideas being put into practice. The meeting of two minds may be explosive, and one or both may think better of the attempt. It may be entirely harmonious; but for most people, achieving that harmony is likely to take a little time – time well spent, when the reward is a companionable, loving relationship. Conflicts may arise over something as trivial as wringing out the dishcloth or as momentous as housing an elderly relative, but the key to resolution is the same – recognising that each person has a legitimate point of view. There are two truths in any relationship.

To go back to Frances, here was someone who had been divorced for some time when the prospect of a new relationship presented itself with Trevor's arrival on the scene. It had been years since she had observed the conventions of her first marriage. Having been single and independent for so long, she had lived life by her own rules. Entering a situation where she thought her own rules would probably be redundant, she felt confused.

It took a wise friend looking at the situation from the outside to help her to see that the person she had become, with all her qualities and experience, was the person to whom Trevor was attracted. Her history spanned time spent as a parent and as a working woman, for a start. She needed the encouragement of a friend to help her to recognise that she had a legitimate right to develop relationships at her own pace. Her example, Gerald's experiences, Grace's story – all show how later-life relationships can give you the chance to rethink your attitudes about what you can and cannot do – and make you open to new possibilities.

NEW LOVE AFTER LOSS

In a large proportion of second marriages made in later life one or both partners have been widowed. The loss of a partner has a profound effect. As is illustrated by the causes of stress on page 17, it is one of the most potent sources. Grief must run its course. To begin with, the days are dull and flat with numbness and shock. There often follows a slow decline into depression before reaching acceptance of the loss. Only after this does it become possible to climb upwards and engage with life again, but the prospect of sliding into misery is so terrifying that some people seek to avoid it by building a bridge to the other side of the chasm. If circumstances dictate, they might throw themselves into work or into taking care of their children. If neither of these distractions present themselves, people for whom loss is compounded by unbearable loneliness may urgently seek a new partner. But the bridge across the divide is made of thin ice, and sooner or later may give way. Putting off the inevitable confrontation with the devastation of loss makes the fall even harder when it comes. Something very similar happens after divorce when people rush into second marriages without working out what went wrong the first time around. Sooner or later the unresolved question surfaces, demanding to be answered. This is often the point at which second marriages crack under the strain.

It takes great courage to deal with loss. It takes time to come to terms with what the loss means for the rest of your life. And anyone going through the experience needs support, from friends and family or from a bereavement counsellor, to enable them to pick up the thread of life again. Those we have lost would want us to live the life remaining to us to the full.

SEX, THE UNSPOKEN LOSS

It is often said that these days the only taboo left is death, now that so much openness and frankness characterises discussion of sex. But one area where sex still seems to be unmentionable is in the context of bereavement. The fact is that if your partner has died, one of the things you will miss is intimacy and sex. To feel a need for sexual release is completely normal, because sexual desire and sexual drive do not just disappear. It seems to be legitimate to express every other kind of loss, but to say 'I miss the sex' is not allowed. This, unsurprisingly, makes it harder to cope with. This attitude persists because people fail to understand the deeper and more complex meanings of sex. If sex is thought of simply as an activity – in other words, no more than the act of intercourse – then the meaning of sex in the lives of loving partners is neglected.

Maggie was sixty-one when Jimmy died of a heart attack. It was the last thing Maggie had expected because Jimmy was so health-conscious and fit. He ate well, took regular exercise and had cut down on his work as a chiropodist. They were as much in love on the day he died as when they married, 'even more so' Jimmy would have said.

In the months that followed Maggie received support from family and friends and was able to talk her grief through with understanding friends. But there was one distressing aspect of her grief that she could not bring herself to share and that was her aching sexual loss. A loss that woke her in the night, reaching out for Jimmy as she would have done in the past. She felt guilty that she had such strong sexual feelings and that she had masturbated to release them. She missed Jimmy so much. She frequently dreamt that they were making love and woke in floods of tears in their empty bed. She became so disturbed by this regular occurrence that she sought sleeping pills from the doctor. She didn't tell him why, just that she was not sleeping. He reassured her that this was a common experience and recommended her to the practice counsellor. She didn't make an appointment immediately but waited several weeks. When she did go it took a couple of sessions before she could bring herself to speak of the part of her grief which was her sexual loss. The counsellor made her feel how normal her feelings were, that she was missing a part of their lives together that had always had a special meaning for them, that every aspect of their relationship needed a place in her grieving for Jimmy, indeed that having sexual feelings was an important way of holding him in her memory.

When it is understood that sex means intimacy, comfort, concern, fulfilment and joy – then it may be possible to acknowledge the magnitude of its loss. We have looked at the stories of two people who felt this effect. On the one hand is Frances, who was inexplicably anxious about embarking on a sexual relationship with her new friend Trevor. One of the factors at play in such situations is the hidden fear that a new relationship will force you to acknowledge that when the previous relationship ended, the loss of sex was an important element. Then there is Gerald, for whom the prospect of losing a new sexual partner produced such anxiety that his very ability to be actively sexual was impaired.

RESPECTING THE PAST

If you are the second partner of someone whose first partner has died, you might worry about measuring up to the memory of that person – even though you know that you are not in any sense a replacement for them. It can be difficult not to idealise the dead to some degree, and it is important to respect the past – but not to venerate it. A balance has to be struck and a degree of sensitivity called for while you strive to find that balance. For example, it would not be reasonable to ask your new partner to banish all photographs of their late husband or wife from your sight any more than it would be tactful for them to cover every surface with mementoes.

The process of dovetailing each other's ideas about life as partners has an added dimension when one partner (or both) has been widowed. When, in the early days, you have a dis- agreement about the way something is done, one of you might think or say, 'That's the way the dear departed would have done it', and feel some restraint about changing things. As mature people with affection for one another, you will have an instinct about what can and can't be done, and when. For example, if you live together in what was the marital home, the newcomer may want to change some of the decorations, especially in the bedroom. He or she may see this as symbolic of a fresh start rather than a denial of the past, and if the other is ready to make a new future they will accept the change for what it is. But suppose the newcomer wants to dig up all the rose-bushes that were planted and cared for by the deceased, and replace them with serviceable evergreens? It might not be so easy to welcome such a move. Practical as it is, it fails to acknowledge the symbolism of the roses. And in doing that, fails to acknowledge appropriately the significance of the past.

Alison and Rob married in their sixties after both had lost their first partners, Bill and Sonia, to cancer. They had met when they had been involved in fundraising for their local town's hospice. Both of their homes had been put on the market before they married so that they could start a new life in a new home. But the market had dipped, and for two years their homes remained unsold. Loath to put in tenants for fear of making the properties less attractive, they spent equal amounts of time in each house. Apart from this setback to their plans, things went well; until Rob decided to 'have a clear-out in Alison's garage'.

After almost two years of sharing homes, Rob didn't think he needed permission to tidy up the garage, and was distressed by the heated row which followed his first trip to the local dump. He had taken an old toolbox full of rusted, unsalvable tools, half a lawnmower and various odd boxes of rubbish. He was completely unprepared for Alison's furious tears and the ensuing silence.

Eventually they were able to talk about the row and how Alison's experience of loss had been re-awakened. The thought of Bill's things, particularly his old toolbox, being consigned to the local tip had triggered unexpected feelings in Alison, feelings that were quite unconnected to her happy new relationship with Rob.

Having two homes had meant that facing a clearing out of the past had been delayed. Rob could see that he might feel the same if Alison had thrown out Sonia's clothes, which were still in a wardrobe in the spare room, without consulting him. Later, the 'clearing out' was something they were able to do together, acknowledging the significance of the memories and associations.

Coming together as new partners in later life, you bring your history with you. It has made you what you are. But you are still being made, still growing as people. Making a new relationship is a statement of hope for the future – like writing the next chapter of your personal history. Through the whole of your life you have been moving on from the past and leaving behind ideas or ways of doing things that you have outgrown. When the way you did things in the past is associated with the person with whom you did them, it can be harder to change them.

Pause for thought

New relationships mean new beginnings and new opportunities.

New beginnings can be thwarted by clinging to the past.

If you are beginning a new relationship, what are you hanging on to from the past that will get in the way of its development?

Expecting doors to be opened? A cup of tea to wake you up? Shirts ironed in a certain way?

Or, more significantly, things your new love cannot hope to compete with – a garage full of old tools, an uncleared wardrobe or a loft full of memorable rubbish?

Chapter Nine

GETTING MORE OUT OF CONVERSATION

Two people who are new to each other in a relation-ship formed in later life will be anxious not to upset each other and will not want to push a claim for change – even in small things. But if they don't find a time and place to talk about them, the two of them can continue with domestic rituals neither of them really enjoy or value just because they think they should. Here is a rather light-hearted example.

Sue went to stay for the weekend with her old friend Angela, who had remarried at the age of fifty-nine about six months earlier. Apart from meeting him at the wedding Sue hardly knew Maurice, Angela's new husband. Before they turned in on the Saturday night, Angela asked Sue if she'd be happy with a big fry-up breakfast the next morning. Sue said she'd prefer something simpler, and Angela agreed with her, saying in a low voice that she'd cook one anyway because Maurice expected it.

Maurice had heard every word of this exchange. It turned out that he had, just the once, said that his late wife always served a huge fried breakfast on Sundays, and Angela had assumed that was what he liked. But he much preferred his usual tea and toast and marmalade, and hadn't wanted to hurt her feelings by saying so. They were still giggling, 'But I thought you . . .' and, 'Why didn't you ask? . . .' as Sue crept upstairs.

If we can find reasons for not bringing into the open some-thing as simple as what to have for breakfast, it's likely that we are going to find ourselves tongue-tied when it comes to more important matters. The importance of communicating well is the subject of this chapter.

Have you ever been in a restaurant and noticed a couple who didn't seem to have anything to say to one another? Once they've ordered their meal and exchanged a few perfunctory words about their surroundings, they seem to lapse into silence. They fiddle with the cutlery or play with the table-linen, not looking into each other's eyes. They're relieved when the food comes and gives them something to do.

Have you ever seen a couple like that and said, 'That's not going to happen to us!'? Or have you just offered up a silent prayer that it never would? What is it about this picture of separateness that causes you to pause for thought? After all, couples who have that distance between them are rarely hostile towards one another. In fact, if you asked them, they would probably say that of course they loved their partner.

Maybe what worries us as spectators is the thought that they are just plain bored with each other. And it might be true. There are other explanations, of course. They may in fact not be a long-term married couple at all, but relatively new to each other and still edging their way towards a closer acquaintance. They may be preoccupied with matters that have nothing to do with their relationship or have had bad news that has left them lost for words.

If boredom is the cause of a less-than-comfortable silence, it might well be because they are one of those couples who have allowed their lives to be ruled by routine. Each of them might have just stopped being curious about the other person. When bustling about at home or rushing off to work a sort of short-hand conversation develops so that the essentials of life can get done. It is all too easy not to notice that the kind of words that keep you close to each other are not being said. When the couple are transplanted to the public space of the restaurant, however, the space between them is plain to see. Just when they should be enjoying an evening out, they feel exposed and uncomfortable, each aggrieved that the other does not appear to be paying them any attention.

Still being able to engage in lively conversation with the person you've been married to for twenty-five years is not something that can be guaranteed. It is something you have to practise in order to keep the sparkle bright. It is easy to slip slowly into a lazy routine of minimal conversation when life is full of the demands of work and family, especially if at the end of every busy day you do nothing more constructive than falling on the couch in front of the television. So easy is it, and so comfortable, that it might not be until circumstances change that you realise something is not quite right. The shorthand-type exchanges that served you just about well enough in run-of-the-mill, day-to-day situations seem to be selling you short when there's a change in your way of life. It often happens at holiday time, when couples have more leisure time together and an expectation of pleasant relaxation. The same situation applies when people retire. If the way you talk to each other isn't as satisfying as it should be, this is when you will have time to notice it.

There is plenty of practical advice available on preparing for retirement. We are told to do what we can to ease the transition from a working life to one where we can do what we like with our time. It is sound advice not to wait until you've been given the gold watch to take up a sport or hobby or to join a club. It is not wise to uproot yourself from a place where you have friends, where you know your way around and which feels familiar, to one you liked because you've had good holidays there. You cannot be sure that a place where you have never spent more than two weeks at a stretch is going to be a congenial spot to spend the rest of your life.

The same applies to talking to each other. It is not easy to acquire the art of meaningful conversation at the age of fifty-plus if you have not been practising it half your life. Even men and women who are starting out on new relationships in later life can find themselves facing gaps in the conversation. As you grow older you acquire a politeness and restraint that holds you back from inquiring too closely about another or revealing too much about yourself too soon. But it is not impossible to fill the conversational gaps, and if you are sufficiently motivated by the awful thought of sitting opposite each other in a restaurant with nothing to say, your chances of making a go of it are so much the greater.

Pause for thought

Are there times when you feel you've got nothing to say to your partner?

Is that because you are comfortable or because you are bored? Have the responses become so predictable that it's not worth having the conversation?

Do you want it to be different?

Only you can make a start. Think about trying this. The next time you are in a pub or restaurant with your partner, invite him or her to join you in speculating about the people around you. Have some fun and give your imagination an airing.

Are that pair in the corner married, or having a torrid affair?

What does the guy at the bar do for a living: lumberjack, offshore rigger, insurance man?

Is the woman on her own waiting for someone?

What's the family party celebrating: a lottery win or someone's birthday?

The permutations are endless.

Situation, situation, situation – according to estate agents, the three most important criteria for buying a house. The couples counsellor's equivalent might well be communication, communication, communication, because this is the only way we can begin to know each other. The impulse to know what it is about the other person that makes them individual and the desire to be known as you really are, are qualities central to the state of loving one another. Research that has been done with partners in relationships which 'work' reveals that being able to talk to each other is of paramount importance.

Falling in love seems to happen naturally without any effort involved. We expect that communicating with each other will come naturally, too – we are under the illusion that, like breathing, this is something we shouldn't have to think about. We've learnt most of the words, so that should be enough. But we have also picked up habits of speech and assumptions about others while acquiring the vocabulary. Later on, those hidden assumptions can get in the way of understanding others and being understood ourselves. Getting to know a person really well and being able to manage situations where conflict arises takes skills that we do not necessarily 'just pick up'. No one takes the trouble to teach us, either. We may be lucky enough to learn by example, but one way or another, if we want these skills we have to learn them.

Think about learning to drive as an example. When you started, you didn't know anything about how a car works or the highway code. You wanted to learn – that's why you'd asked your mum or dad to teach you or booked lessons with an instructor. With a mixture of excitement and apprehension you got behind the wheel for the first time. By the end of the lesson you were beginning to be aware of just how much you didn't know – how difficult it is to steer and change gear at the same time as well as checking your rear-view mirror.

It takes not one but several lessons and hours of practice before you can perform these actions competently. With each new technique you learned, you seemed to go backwards to a state of ignorance again – stalling as you drove up a hill, crashing the gears on an awkward bend, climbing up on the pavement when you should have been turning the car in the road. As you practised it got easier and your driving skills improved. You were ready to take your test at the point when you knew what you had to do and believed yourself to be competent enough.

By the time you had passed your test and were out on the road – in charge of the car, sure of the direction you were travelling in and respectful of other drivers – you were no longer self-conscious about what you were doing. You had achieved a level of competence which was both challenged and constantly perfected by being on the road every day. Now, when something unexpected happens, you have what feels like an instinctive capability to deal with it. But the point is that it is not instinctive. You learned it, you practised it, and you put a lot of effort into it. Acquiring the skills of good communication is just like this.

There are situations where the level of communication can be relatively superficial and still be effective – that is, good enough to let people get on with each other – explaining something that needs doing at work, making a dentist's appointment, buying a train ticket. All of these things you can do without necessarily reaching a profound understanding of the other person taking part in the transaction. You don't have to like people to get on with them, and you do have to get on with them, because the alternative is a life marked by hostility and unpleasantness. Getting on with others is made possible by talking and listening with respect, attention and courtesy.

Respect, attention and courtesy are vital in our intimate relationships too, but to a greater degree and at a deeper level. And we must add that element of curiosity about the other person and the wish to be intimately close that impels us to make the effort to understand and be understood.

When you first fall in love, part of the miracle seems to be that you have so many hopes and dreams and attitudes in common with the other person. There doesn't seem to be enough time to talk about all the things you want to share; you feel like two halves of a whole, and the more you are with the other person the more 'right' the fit seems to be. This is the period when each has stars (or smoke) in their eyes; the time when you hear people say they are 'crazy about each other'. Physical attraction is strong and emotions passionate.

It has to cool down some time, and in the next stage the process of really getting to know the other person and to reveal your true self to them begins. Sometimes that is as far as it gets, if you don't like what you find. For relationships that blossom and continue, however, it is the beginning of a journey.

If the journey of life is not without its twists and turns, nor is the process of getting to know another person to whom you have committed yourself always very comfortable. The person you imagined to be perfect and in perfect harmony with you turns out to be imperfect and to have different opinions about things. You discover things about which you cannot be wholeheartedly enthusiastic; you reveal things about yourself which the other person isn't crazy about either, and you have to face the fact of your own imperfections. But other characteristics come to light that are unique and precious: things you each do or say which the other person delights in. You support each other through the ups and downs; you help each other to reach the goals you've set for yourselves. You begin to build a relationship based on reality, not fantasy.

In the last chapter we looked at how the need to deal with the inevitable changes of life means being willing to negotiate and renegotiate. Doing this brings rewards at more than one level. As they get better at negotiating with each other, couples can learn more about each other, too. Realising that there is always more to learn about the person you share your life with is one of the elements that keeps that relationship fresh. Suppose there is a disagreement about what to do with your holiday time. In debating the relative merits of staying at home doing nothing, or landscaping the garden, or lying on a beach in Spain, much can be discovered about attitudes to money and time, for example. These are two issues that, if unexplored, often cause couples to fall out. Openness, courage and honesty are crucial to any discussion about life's big issues, and can make it possible to snatch benefits even from adverse situations.

James and Kathryn are a couple who were in their mid-forties when circumstances forced fairly major changes in their lifestyle, and could have left their family in tatters. James came from a wealthy landowning family, and had met his wife Kathryn when he was at agricultural college. She was a nursing student at the time and carried on working until their first child, a daughter, was born. They lived a conventional English country life. Three daughters arrived in quick succession, all of whom later went to private schools, as the children in James's family had always done. James was busy with estate management and family business matters. They entertained a fair bit and Kathryn became a cordon bleu cook. What with the WI and the parish council and so on they were both involved in local community life, too.

James and Kathryn came from very different backgrounds. The oldest of five children, he had grown up in the country with little supervision from his parents, who took a robust attitude to their offspring. Family meals were large, noisy affairs with a lot of chatting and laughing. Everyone was given a job to do and all the children got used to sharing tasks and problems. The big old house was a bit shabby and not always immaculately clean, but welcoming and friendly. Having said that, it could be difficult to be seen as an individual.

Kathryn and her younger brother had been brought up in the county town where James had been to college. Her father, who had worked on the railways, and her mother, a dressmaker, were a quiet, hardworking couple who had struggled to buy their home when they were young parents. They took great pride in their house and garden; everything was as neat and clean as a new pin. In this well-ordered household, the children were expected to keep their bedrooms tidy, come to the table on time with their hands washed, and work hard at school. The parents spent most weekends tidying up the garden or doing a spot of painting and decorating. They never seemed to argue about anything and were disapproving if Kathryn and her brother fell out over a game or who could have the kaleidoscope. They were obviously pleased when Kathryn got into nursing school and her brother did well at his A-levels. But displays of enthusiasm were not their style.

Warm as her welcome into James's family was, it took Kathryn a while to get used to their way of doing things. He loved the calmness of her nature, and the way in which she gave him a sense that all her attention was on him. She was frankly dazzled by his confidence and sense of fun, which gave her the freedom to be more expressive than she had dared to be in her youth. But breaking the habits of a lifetime proved easier said than done, and to start with James would some-times get exasperated by Kathryn's reluctance to challenge him on anything. For her part, she sometimes felt invaded by the cheerful disregard for privacy that he and his family took for granted. It got to the point where James would deliberately provoke Kathryn to see if he could make her angry. It was only when she burst into desperate sobs one time that – when things had calmed down – they tried to work out what was really going on.

James tried to explain that when she was quiet, it felt as if she had turned away from him. He was used to having to fight hard to be heard. Kathryn explained that even when she was quiet, she really was still 'with him', but at the same time found it difficult to speak up for herself for fear of attracting disapproval. After that, they made a pact. In future Kathryn would do her very best to speak up if she wasn't happy about something, however trivial it seemed to be. James would do his best not to jump to the wrong conclusions about her quiet moments, and go on the attack.

When their eldest daughter was fourteen, a series of misfor-tunes left James, through no fault of his own, unexpectedly fac-ing enormous family debts. It looked as if everything would have to change: the house would have to be sold, the girls taken out of school, heirlooms auctioned off. They were faced with a crisis of the kind that, without the resources they had to draw on, can provoke suicide or divorce. They endured some very difficult times during which their pledge was seriously put to the test.

After two years of hardship and stress their life was very different; a much smaller house, local school for the girls, a little van instead of a big estate car, which Kathryn used for the catering business she had started. James caught a train to Bristol every morning, where he had found a job.

The resources that James and Kathryn had to draw on had nothing to do with money, but came from the way in which, over the years, they made sure they stayed 'in touch' with each other come what may. Habits developed when times were good stood them in good stead when the going got tough. Simple enough things like always giving each other a hug and a kiss when they went their separate ways in the morning were tiny but important messages of encouragement to get them through the day. And every evening, after the meal had been eaten and the dishes put away, they spent half an hour together without interruptions from the children, the television or the telephone, just talking. They would each start with 'Tell me one bad thing about your day' and try to get it into perspective. They would each end with 'Tell me one good thing about your day', aiming to finish it on a hopeful note. There were times when Kathryn found it difficult to speak and James could only rage about what had happened, but they never missed what they called 'our time'. Looking back, they say that those times did a lot to help them to pull through and to feel they were 'in it together'.

Chapter Ten

BREACHES OF TRUST

Trust between the two partners in a marriage or relationship is crucial. It is not an instantaneous gift bestowed on new lovers but is built up over time as two people get to know each other. It is one of the most important factors in the 'fit' between a man and a woman who make a commitment to be true to each other. Partly this is because what constitutes trust for one couple may not be the same as for another – in practice a process of finding out about the other person's beliefs and attitudes has to take place before we can feel confident about getting closer to them.

The ideas we have about trust in adulthood have been forming all our lives. Those of us who have always been secure in the love of our parents and family may be more optimistic about the likelihood of being dealt with fairly by other people than will those who have experienced loss in childhood or who have had to struggle for attention. Some people are brought up with a very strict code of behaviour which makes it difficult for them to accept other, more easy-going, ways of living. One way or another we will all have taken on board in our formative years a clutch of ideas about what it is right to expect of other people and what we ought to give in return. Often these ideas become a part of who we are almost unconsciously; sometimes we question their validity and construct new ideas for ourselves. As we make the tentative steps towards forming what we hope will be the most significant relationship of our lives, we find ways of discovering how our ideas fit in with those of the other person.

It is a fitting together rather than an exact match that works. One partner may have to relax their 'rules' as the other convinces him or her of their irrelevance. This can apply to everyday matters like always being home at the same time from work or bigger issues like wanting to go away for a weekend with a group of like-minded friends. Some women would be horrified at the idea of their husband going off rock-climbing with his mates, just as some men would strongly resist the idea of their wife going on a weekend cookery course with her girlfriends. As time goes by, however, each learns that there is no threat to the relationship in their partner's wish to pursue their interests independently, and balances the time spent apart with good times together.

As can be seen from the chart on page 41, by the time couples have reached forty, jealousy is very low down the list of potential sources of conflict. Research carried out with a group of couples who had been together for more than fifty years showed that those who were classified as 'happy' treated each other with respect, politeness and kindness. Respecting each other's differences might be thought to be part of that. Furthermore, these couples had learned how to manage comfortable levels of intimacy and distance in their marriages. In terms of building up and nurturing trust between each other, this is highly significant.

Not all the fifty-year marriages in the research study were happy; in some cases an emotional and physical distance lay between the partners, but they had stayed together either because of strong religious beliefs or because divorce was unacceptable to them. Financial security was also a factor among the women. In these marriages, the partners were apparently still physically together but mentally a long way apart.

If you trust someone, you are not afraid to get close to them or to let them get close to you. Conversely, if you are afraid of closeness, it will be difficult to start to build trust and to keep it alive. A fine balance has to be struck – between each individual's need for intimacy and distance and the way that fluctuating need meshes in with the needs of their partner. It is a never-ending dance: sometimes moving seamlessly together, sometimes gliding apart. As long as each one pays attention to the rhythm and is conscious of the other's steps, nobody trips up. To put it more prosaically, successful relationships depend on each partner remaining aware of the other person's needs: for that to happen, they have to talk to each other and listen to each other. Each will do their best not to take the other for granted.

The longer a marriage has lasted, the more likely it is to continue. That does not mean to say that long-term marriages run themselves or that breaches of hard-earned trust do not take place. The sense of hurt that follows the discovery of a betrayal can be intense.

Sheila and Ted had been married for thirty-four years when the bombshell hit their marriage and she discovered that Ted had been 'having an affair' with someone at work. To be fair, Ted was as amazed at his own behaviour as Sheila. 'The affair', in fact, had been a one-off sexual liaison with a divorcee in his department. It happened while they were away on the same two-day management team-building event.

Ted worked for a large multinational engineering company, recently taken over by an American conglomerate. He was coming towards the end of his career and was keen to maximise his pension, so that he and Sheila would have a comfortable retirement. He was working hard to continue to impress his new bosses. Sheila had given up work when the children came along and had always enjoyed her role as home-maker and now grandmother. They had a firm circle of friends and a regular, well-organised life.

Sheila's and Ted's sexual relationship was regular, too. Passion had long ago been lost to routine but it suited them like an old, familiar slipper: comforting, if a bit dull. Two years prior to the bombshell, Sheila had had a hysterectomy, followed by a lengthy convalescence. Naturally, sex was, in

Ted's words, 'out of the question for a time'. There was an extensive period of abstinence followed eventually by infrequent love-making because Sheila suffered some soreness after penetration. Ted, not wanting to cause Sheila pain, assumed the problem was caused by the surgery and – well, 'That was that.'

Sheila's doctor had mentioned the likelihood of such problems in the post-operative consultations but she had found the conversations embarrassing and had not sought further advice. Sheila and Ted themselves never really talked about the problem. Sheila did not mind not having sex so much because of the pain, but she missed the cuddles and the closeness. For his part, Ted missed regular sex much more. He found himself having sexual dreams and increasing numbers of morning erections.

At work, Liz, a recently divorced forty-four-year-old computer expert, brought in to upgrade Ted's department's IT, seemed to single him out for special attention. At first he thought it was because he was head of the section. Gradually, however, he became aware that he had begun to fantasise about her.

Two drinks too many after dinner on the first evening of the management training event found him in her bed acting out those fantasies. Hours later he stole back to his own room, feeling guilty, ashamed and shocked at what had happened.

When Ted got home it didn't take a Sherlock Holmes to make it clear to Sheila that something was not right with him. For a brief few weeks he sustained his silence about what had happened but as the days passed and Liz continued to make more and more moves in his direction at work, he felt less and less able to counter them. He decided the only way forward was to confess to Sheila, ask her forgiveness and get back to normal. After all, it was only one offence in a lifetime.

The trouble was, he hadn't anticipated Sheila's reaction. She went ballistic; angry and tearful by turns. Hostile and aggressive one minute, hurt and weeping the next. Sheila was in shock. She felt betrayed, bewildered, rejected, punished and, at some level, that it must have been her fault. She couldn't sleep in the same bed as Ted, she couldn't talk to him, she couldn't stop crying. She was devastated. The aftermath of this one event seemed to go on and on. Sheila felt her confidence and trust in Ted had taken a body-blow of unexpected proportions. She constantly felt in need of reassurance of his love but when he gave it she didn't feel any better. Ted was despairing of his inability to comfort his wife and make it all right again.

Sheila, who had never been one for pursuing conversation, now found herself wanting details of what had happened, how he had felt, what 'she' was like. She experienced intense feelings of rage and jealousy towards this woman, who she saw as destroying their lives. She wanted to know everything, including, when it occurred to her in the middle of one night, waking Ted to ask whether the sex had been protected. Suddenly Sheila realised there was more at risk than the marriage. Ted explained that it was Liz who had produced and insisted on a condom being used. He, not anticipating the event, had been ill-prepared.

Thankful that at least safe sex had been practised, Sheila and Ted began to get their lives back together. Ted went to work, always promising every morning to minimise contact with Liz, whose role in his department was coming to an end in any case. Sheila got on with their regular routine, watchful, over the storm, although still not able to understand why Ted had done what he had. In some strange way it was Ted's ill-preparedness that had begun to dissipate Sheila's anger and to allow her to look at her part in the process. Sheila thought long and hard about their lives over the last two years. She realised that she had let go of their sexual relationship because she had been unwilling to get help for herself.

She took the bull by the horns and went back to see the doctor about the pain during sex which had plagued her since the hysterectomy. She was prescribed HRT and given advice about vaginal lubrications. It all seemed so easy and she was angry with herself for not having done it much earlier. It was

Sheila who initiated the return of the sexual relationship. The relief was great for both of them.

With hindsight, Ted and Sheila began to see Ted's infidelity for what it was – an indication that things weren't right, a catalyst to sorting out their lost intimate closeness since the hysterectomy, an opportunity to realise how much they had come to take their relationship for granted. This painful time produced important improvements in their relationship on a number of levels, not least of which was an appreciation of just how much they valued it.

AFTER AN AFFAIR

The immediate legacy of discovering that your partner has had an affair is a set of feelings not unlike those that occur with any loss – in this case, loss of trust. As well as feeling shocked and angry, you may feel terribly confused. Your expectations of your life as one half of a couple have been gravely disappointed; if you cannot believe in this, what else can you believe in? It is as if all the signposts have been turned round the wrong way. Emotionally you feel completely disoriented. Underlying this confusion is the inability to understand why the unthinkable has happened. Coming to understand why is important, because it is the first step in the process of healing.

Once the initial shock had begun to subside, Sheila took the time to think about the situation that had arisen and to take action that would ensure a better future for her and Ted. She understood that 'the affair' with Liz was a symptom with a number of causes.

There are danger points in relationships where, if circumstances permit, one partner might be tempted to seek a way out by having an affair – only to realise that affairs are not solutions. Part of being prepared for the changes of mid-life and later life, for example, means recognising that your partner will not be the same person for ever. The fact that you change as time goes by and have to adapt to different circumstances is one of the things that makes you interesting to each other. It is disheartening to feel taken for granted, and in a desperate bid to get attention when all attempts at communication have failed, people have been known to embark on an affair – with scant attempt to conceal it – in the hope of being noticed.

It might come at forty, or fifty or even later, but all of us reach a point where we want to take stock of our lives; there is a feeling that some people express as reaching a fork in the road. You look back on your past life and try to make some sense of it. You look forward and try to figure out how to manage the years ahead. Inevitably there will be some unfulfilled ambitions, some dreams that did not come true. Some people will be seized with a sense of panic that their chances are slipping away, and in this state cast around for new experiences – and an affair or fling could be just that experience. When it is over, however, reality is still there waiting to be dealt with – only now it is more complicated because your partner has been hurt and you may not like yourself very much for involving a third person (however willing they might have seemed) and moved on.

Some long-term marriages are surprisingly able to contain and accept infidelity, until the unspoken 'rules' are broken. It was just such a case for Hilary and Geoffrey. Hilary knew that Geoffrey had affairs and had tolerated them throughout their married life because Geoffrey only ever 'played away from home'. He travelled a lot for his job and his relationships never really threatened the marriage. Hilary accepted that Geoffrey needed to have relationships with other women, but that he always came safely back to base. It was not until Hilary went to visit her sister in Canada for a month that Geoffrey broke the unspoken rules about his behaviour. Geoffrey 'entertained' his latest conquest at home and in the marital bed.

When Hilary got home from Canada the next door neighbour couldn't wait to let her know about the strange car in the drive and the strange woman who drove it. Hilary challenged

Geoffrey and he, not thinking it was of any great significance, admitted that he had brought someone home. What Geoffrey had done was 'sully the nest' and this was unforgiveable in Hilary's book. Not only was she embarrassed at the neighbour's disclosure, but furious at Geoffrey's casual dismissal of what he had done by having sex with someone else in their bed. It took her six weeks of torment before she finally consulted a solicitor and petitioned for divorce.

This was one instance of a lack of real communication between a couple paving the way for disaster. Not keeping in touch with each other's thoughts and feelings was behind what happened to Kevin and Susan, too. Kevin worked long hours, leaving Susan very much to her own devices most evenings. Susan, at fifty-three, her parenting days over, found herself increasingly unhappy at how little time they had together and how Kevin seemed to value his job more than their marriage. She surprised herself when she responded to the advances of a friend's husband. She was amazed at how easy it was to have a clandestine relationship when your husband was hardly there.

It took a year before Kevin found out about the affair and another year before the awful acrimony between them brought them to Relate. Lack of communication brought about painful consequences – overwhelming feelings of betrayal were compounded by jealousy and possessiveness. It took many months to rebuild the trust between them and it was difficult for them to believe that their relationship could ever be the same again. And they were right. When an affair is discovered, relationships go 'into shock'. Something has happened that inevitably means that you can't go back to how it was. Indeed, if you try to, then you're only papering over the cracks and not dealing with the issues that promoted the affair in the first place. After an affair, couples need to see that they have an opportunity to re-evaluate their relationship – to make it different. They need to renegotiate the ground rules and their expectations of each other, so that they may begin to regain confidence and trust in each other.

Chapter Eleven

GETTING CLOSER

To misquote the old song, sex is where you find it: look around – it's all round you, everywhere. A quick survey of women's magazines in the local newsagents furnished the following lines:

'Do you + him = great sex?'
'Six ways to get what you want tonight'
'The chat-up lines that got 22 women into bed'

The men's magazine section provided these:

'Make beautiful women swoon'
'Seven secrets of raunchy sex'
'Six-babe pile-up'

You would be forgiven for thinking that people are so busy having sex or reading about it that they never have time for anything else. What's more, the impression is that the sex everyone is having is *wonderful* sex. On top of that, all of these magazines are clearly aimed at a readership aged thirty-five or below. Apparently the rest of us are too busy gardening or decorating or fixing cars to be interested in sex – the message is, sex is the preserve of the young and beautiful. There is also an unspoken assumption that in order to be enjoying a sex life, men and women must not only be young but also beautiful.

AGEISM

It usually takes a little time for the human face to acquire the qualities that will make it interesting. Real beauty has depth and staying power. As the poet Keats put it, it 'is a joy forever. Its loveliness increases'. Or as a modern American put it rather less poetically, young good looks often 'front an empty lot'.

To set a value on people because of the way they look is as offensive as it is to judge them because of their colour or nationality. Ageism actually degrades young people who fall victim to it, since in theory once their youth has passed they will condemn themselves to a meaningless half life. In practice the boundaries of youth are always shifting. From the perspective of eighty, to be forty seems young. From the perspective of children under ten, thirty seems ancient. These days you can even buy birthday cards with a detachable badge proclaiming '50 is the new 30'.

The unfounded assumption that youth bestows value on people gets applied to both men and women. To complicate matters, society has different ideas about what signals sexual competence for each of the sexes. Broadly speaking, men have been given the message that they should be sexually *active* – that is, strong and virile: 'Build powerful shoulders' comes the order from the men's magazines.

Women have traditionally been encouraged to be sexually *attractive*, according to whatever ideal of feminine beauty is currently in vogue. The Edwardians liked their women voluptuous but with tiny waists; by the 1920s boyish figures were the rage; Marilyn Monroe, who had half the male population at her feet, was a dress size 16; 1990s icons Gwyneth Paltrow and Kate Moss look like waifs. Whatever the current physical ideal, headlines from contemporary women's magazines show that sexual assertiveness is beginning to be a feature of young women's behaviour in the 1990s.

In themselves the factors that make men and women attractive to each other are important in ensuring the continuance of the human race. Ideas about what constitutes good looks are subject to fashion – they come and they go. Whether you have straight or curly hair, long legs, wide hips or broad shoulders – these are genetic accidents. Taken to extremes, and in the context of individuals' lives, the pursuit of physical ideals alone does not promote love and intimacy.

The truth is that sexuality – the real thing – is a quality that transcends the superficial. Sexuality is often confused in our society with sexual activity. But sexuality or sexiness is an aspect of personality. It is not something to fear as an untamed part of your being that could take you over. Those who are most comfortable with this aspect of themselves can communicate their sexuality from within without fear of being misinterpreted. To acknowledge your own sexuality and to take responsibility for its expression in an intimate partnership is vital to all healthy relationships.

And that expression takes many forms: focusing all your attention on your partner, making them laugh, pulling their leg, captivating them in conversation, being able to make them feel as if they are the only person in the world, enjoying touching and being touched. Sexiness is in a deep gaze, tender words softly spoken, laughter shared, a sensuous touch, and giving and taking. Sexuality doesn't start to fade on your twenty-ninth birthday or even when you get your bus pass. It becomes integrated into your life over time – it is not an add-on extra. The pleasure afforded by your sexuality comes not only from the sex act and the 'performance' – but is there all the time, informing all your actions. It is part of you.

Alfred Kinsey, the famous researcher into human sexual behaviour of the late 1950s, did his bit to reinforce the idea that sex was the almost exclusive preserve of the young. Kinsey, who established the Kinsey Institute in 1947, interviewed 12,000 people, of whom only 186 were over sixty. Only seven of the 16,000 pages of his report refer to sexuality in this age group. He rendered them virtually invisible.

Masters & Johnson, pioneers of sex therapy a decade later, did little to rescue our forebears from oblivion. Only thirty-one people in this age range were interviewed for their large study. The inference that if young equals sexually active, then not-young equals sexually inert, was made. The effects of that theory are still being felt. Look again at the story of Gerald, who at sixty-plus found new love only to be roundly condemned by his grown-up daughter, Claire. By displaying distaste and disapproval of her father's physical relationship with Elaine, she was accepting an unproven hypothesis about human sexuality which would mean that she would, in time, be obliged to deny herself the abiding pleasure of sex with her partner. Let's hope she becomes enlightened before her half-century, because sex is *not* just for the young.

Eric and Nancy are a couple who proved this for themselves. Before they met, they would have described themselves as very conventional and not in the least given to romantic notions. They had both been widowed for some years and had fairly settled routines in their lives. They were both fit and healthy and in their early sixties. Eric had been a member of the local Ramblers' Association for a number of years when Nancy joined, encouraged by a friend. She came to enjoy the Saturday walks very much, looking forward to the social chat as much as the walking and often finding herself accompanied by Eric. They shared a lot of common interests and conversation was easy.

Uncharacteristically, Nancy found herself suggesting to Eric that he come for Sunday lunch one week. He accepted and turned up looking very gallant, with a bottle of wine and a potted geranium out of his greenhouse. He admired her garden and her cooking and they discovered they had similar tastes in music. The lunch was a great success and over the next few months became a regular event, each taking turns to host the meal.

Nancy was surprised at how sexually attractive she found Eric. She had long ago given up any ideas of a new sexual partner. She felt her sexuality had ebbed away slowly as she nursed her sick husband to his death. She was a bit disconcerted when she began to find Eric in her dreams, dreams that were distinctly sexual.

Eric, for his part, was having a similar experience. He was finding Nancy very attractive but felt awkward about showing it. He felt out of practice and afraid of making a fool of himself. Eric wanted more than just the goodbye peck on the cheek that had become their habit, but he felt gauche and unsophisticated, despite his years.

He determined to make a move. He decided he would make dinner rather than lunch for Nancy on her birthday and would be more obviously affectionate. When the evening came, dinner and wine produced a mellow mood, and Frank Sinatra added the finishing touches. They sat next to each other on the sofa having coffee and Eric kissed Nancy 'for real' as he had planned.

They were both surprised at the passion that broke through with that first real contact. They caught their breath at their reaction to each other's touch. They described themselves later as being like romping teenagers, eager and willing.

Sex with their previous partners had never been much to write home about. It was something that happened regularly and was enjoyable, but it had not prepared them for what they were now feeling. Nancy stayed the night and found out, as they embraced again in the morning, that it hadn't just been the wine.

Both of them felt that they had been given a remarkable second chance. They had discovered for themselves that sex is not just for the young.

Our generation, whose knowledge about sex was hard-won, deserves at the very least acceptance of our continuing sexuality in later years. A movement of resistance against sexual ageism is called for. Much research (see page 147) dispels the idea that only the young have a right to sexual expression. More than that, it proves that – given the chance – older people go right ahead and claim their rights. This is just as it should be, because our need to be touched and to be intimate does not diminish with age.

EXPLODING THE MYTHS

Turn to the problem pages inside the magazines and you will read how troubled many people are because of ignorance about sex, confusion about their bodies and anxiety about personal performance. Paradoxically, such anxiety is likely to be aggravated by being invited to make comparisons between our own sex lives and those that we see and hear about in the media.

Achieving and maintaining sexual contentment in later-life relationships happens in a context in which myth and fantasy about what 'good sex' is are mixed up with real-life experiences of a different order. Those aged fifty plus have also been subject to a particular collection of myths, especially about the proper roles of men and women. This is a good stage in life to start clearing some of them out of the way.

Do you notice how numbers feature in the magazine strap-lines? As if it is quantity, not quality that is the measure of satisfying sexual relationships – the printed equivalent of notches on the bedpost. If what we see in the media were a truthful reflection of people's sexual lives, then the only people enjoying a sex life would be the young and beautiful. Worse than that, sexual passion in the old is either thought to be non-existent or condemned. The same behaviour and needs that are applauded as virile and lusty in young men are looked upon as lechery if exhibited by their fathers and uncles. Older women are expected to grow old gracefully, which seems to mean wearing boring mud-coloured clothes and disappearing into the background. The message from the media is that if you have wrinkles, you are past it.

Numbers can be useful, however, when they give us important information about what is really going on in the sexual lives of older people. Some research conducted in the US by Edward M. Brecher took as subjects about 4,500 people aged between fifty and eighty. The research gave a very clear indication that older people are undoubtedly involved in sexual relationships, thank you very much, and put paid to the notion that being over fifty means being over the hill. The main reason for restricted sexual activity in older people is not lack of desire and interest, but lack of opportunity, as a consequence of being divorced or widowed.

If current demographic predictions are proved correct, people past retirement age are in line to make up almost a quarter of the population by 2031. Furthermore, the huge improvement in life expectancy this century means that women can now expect to enjoy thirty more years of healthy life after the menopause. And in the period from 1971 to 1991 life expectancy for men who had reached sixty increased by 2.4 years. The last time that happened it took not twenty but as many as seventy years, from 1900 to 1970, to execute the same improvement. All the indications are that increases in life expectancy will continue. What this means is not just that people are living longer, but they are more likely to be in a couple relationship in their later years.

At the beginning of the twentieth century, it was relatively rare for a couple to celebrate their twenty-fifth wedding anniversary. There were more of them in the 1930s, and now the silver wedding party is commonplace (and often quite raucous). People who married in the 1950s and 1960s can fully expect to live long enough to celebrate their fortieth wedding anniversary. Keeping a sexual relationship healthy and fresh over that number of years doesn't just happen: both partners have to work at it: there is familiarity, tolerance and acceptance, but you also have to watch for complacency and boredom.

LEARNING ABOUT SEX

In the early part of the twentieth century most of the available information about sexual matters was inaccurate and misleading. Any sexual activity not associated with procreation was thought of as bad if not downright dangerous. The dire threats of venereal disease and illegitimacy were raised to frighten youngsters out of engaging in anything sexual.

In the 1920s and 1930s the notion that masturbation could cause mental illness was held as a truth by many medics. Many a marriage manual said so. The 1930 edition of Baden Powell's *Scouting for Boys* still preached fervently against masturbation, warning that it was the cause of many ills. It was called 'the secret vice', and considered a serious disease.

In the post-Victorian era women were expected to be chaste and not to seek sexual gratification for themselves – only to provide it for their husbands. Generally accepted medical opinion at the time held that women did not masturbate, unless they were demented. It was thought that in order to remain well, women should be free of sexual passion. Ironically, in the Victorian era that gave rise to these ideas, prostitution was rampant and London was the pornography capital of the world.

None of today's readers will remember these benighted times. But we were brought up by parents who were much closer to them, and however liberated we may hope to be, it can take a great deal of effort to throw off entirely the effects of early family messages about sex and sexuality.

What ideas and expectations about sex do those of us who grew up in the 1950s and 1960s bring to our late adulthood? The information given to girls about sex was more often than not woefully inadequate, and what was taught was usually based on the anatomy of the rabbit rather than of human beings. It was the female rabbit, at that; those who wanted to find out how the buck played his part were in for a long wait. While the girls were getting less than half the story in biology lessons, the boys were sharing what little they knew at the back of the bike shed. One of them might have got hold of a sex manual. In it they would find chapters with such inspiring titles as 'Patience with a young bride' that implied that all the responsibility for the success of the endeavour lay with the man – and that you really knew what the endeavour was all about, when in fact ignorance was commonplace.

For many, coyness and properness prevented the exchange of knowledge and inevitably threw a veil of shame over human sexual activity. To the sense of shame was added an element of danger. Everyone will have their tale to tell of bizarre attempts by teachers or parents to protect their virtue. At one girls' school the pupils were sent to the annual dance at the boys' school equipped with a folded newspaper – no, not to smack any over-ambitious lad on the wrist, but to put between her bottom and his knee on the ride home in a shared taxi. For some boys, it was the evils of masturbation that were invoked to frighten the life out of them. It was common to be warned that 'self-abuse' would lead to all sorts of debilitation, including blindness or warts on the back of hands at best and compulsive paedophilia at worst!

In Hollywood, the Hays code – which was in force until 1960 – dictated that married couples in films should always have twin beds, be buttoned up to the neck in pyjamas and keep one foot on the floor (unmarried couples getting anywhere near a bedroom scene was unthinkable, unless one of them was confined to bed because of illness). How it was that so many of these screen couples managed to produce broods of shining children remains a mystery.

Pause for thought

Be honest with yourself: what was the real extent of your sex education?

The reproductive system of the frog or rabbit in school biology classes?

The purple prose of the Bible, where everyone was 'begetting' and women were 'taken in adultery'?

A well-thumbed copy of *Lady Chatterley's Lover?*

Bragging around the back of the bicycle sheds?

Young fumblings in the abandoned Anderson shelter?

Can you be sure that the marriage manual you read thirty years ago would stand up to examination now?

Divorce, adultery, sex before marriage and cohabitation attracted sharp disapproval. Boys who made their girlfriends pregnant were expected to make 'honest women' of them through marriage. Women who enjoyed flirting with men were labelled 'fast'. Divorcees were almost by definition in this category, and if not fast were probably 'gay', which simply meant out for a good time. The word for male homosexuals was 'queer', and practising homosexuals were breaking the law. It wasn't until 1967 that the Sexual Offences Act following from the Wolfenden report changed all that – at least for consenting adults over twenty-one.

As the twentieth century entered its second half, a social revolution took place that has affected all of us, even if at the time many of us were more likely to be observers rather than participants. The austerity of the war years was replaced by abundance. We learned that we had never had it so good. Christian Dior's 1947 New Look, which meant using yards of cloth to make a single skirt, was overtaken twenty years later by Mary Quant's miniskirt, exposing inches of female thigh never before seen on the high street. The soldier's Brylcreemed short back and sides grew to shoulder-length locks. We were told to make love, not war. Males who heeded Timothy Leary's dictum to 'tune in, turn on and drop out' wore silk and frills and bright colours. Even chaps in sober suits started wearing gaudy ties. Their girlfriends burnt their bras and went on the pill (without telling their mothers).

It's difficult to say whether it was simply the risk of unwanted pregnancy or the damage that becoming sexually active would do to a girl's reputation which was the most powerful brake on behaviour before the days of reliable contraception. The fact is that even for married women, who had in the eyes of contemporary society achieved respectability, unwanted pregnancy was a serious problem. Repeated pregnancies took their toll on women's health, as did caring for numerous children on a single wage that was stretched further with each new arrival. Before the Abortion Law Reform Act in

1968, abortion was illegal. But desperate women paid for clumsy 'backstreet' abortions which sometimes killed them and sometimes left them infertile. Men who visited prostitutes ran the risk of picking up a sexually transmitted disease. As well as having adverse effects on their own health there was a potential risk to their wives.

Getting reliable information about sex wasn't easy for young men and women growing up in those years. A few might have been given the facts by enlightened parents for whom talking to their children about sex was not taboo. Others will have got a bit of the jigsaw from a friend here, another bit from a big brother or sister there, giving a personal and possibly inaccurate interpretation of the facts. Others will have secretly consulted a medical dictionary and shocked themselves into terrified celibacy. Literature is full of accounts by turns tragic and hilarious of the way in which men and women of our generation learned about what was euphemistically called the birds and the bees. Many of our generation started to gather their information about sex when they were in their twenties and thirties. Alex Comfort's *Joy of Sex* was a revelation to the pre- and post-war generations when it was first published in 1972 and became a bestseller. But these books were not left lying on the coffee table or openly read on the train – they were more likely to be tucked away in your underwear drawer. Even now, at the supposedly liberated end of the century, sex education is a fraught issue.

Part of the problem of growing old is that you do not expect to need educating about sex. By the time you've reached sixty, say, you should know all about it. After all, you've been doing it long enough!

It is easy to fall prey to the myth that older people do not need information about sex and sexual behaviour. It is an extension of the ageist myth that older people are not interested in sex. Set against the myths some recent research. American Edward Brecher and his colleagues looked at the interests and concerns of people in the age range fifty–ninety-three. When they analysed the questionnaires that had been returned to them, they found to their surprise that: 'Relatively few of our respondents, it turned out, wanted to write about religion in later years, or about transportation problems after the age of fifty. What interested them most – and what they wrote about most eloquently and at greatest length – was, quite simply, love and sexuality.'

If we allow ourselves to go along with ageist propaganda about sex, we may well condemn ourselves to limited lives. What we must demand as we grow older – and particularly when we enter a period in which our sexual needs are changing – is accurate information so that we can continue to lead sexually satisfying lives.

Many of us who grew up with poor information about sex have come to realise how much nonsense we learned. As adults, for the most part we have not allowed it to affect our sex lives save for initial fumbling embarrassments as we began a sexual relationship.

This may be fine while the healthy vigour of the sex drive of adult life is strong enough to defeat the messages of the past. But when that urgent sex drive slows down with age; when we find ourselves in bed with a familiar life partner who, like us, is struggling to understand their sexual changes; then we may need to revisit our store of information. Sexagenarians might find some appropriate and accurate sex education useful.

Indeed it is essential that all who enter the last decades of their lives recognize their need for information about the sexual roads they have never travelled before. Without proper information, particularly about sex, it is possible to be misled by all sorts of misunderstandings and misconceptions which can in their turn lead to unhappiness between partners.

Ignorance about sex is an unnecessary obstacle to the full expression of love in a relationship. It is never too late to get yourself some education, however. This is what Joyce thought when she enrolled on a workers' education programme – in

English Literature, not sex! – after she retired from work. It was something she had always promised herself she would do. Her fellow students were a lively bunch and the lecturer a bit of a feminist. The reading was challenging in more ways than one. Joyce found herself reading books that had sexually explicit passages. She found herself reading about sexual experiences of a kind she had not known in her own marriage. She had never experienced an orgasm and until now it hadn't bothered her. The idea that it would be nice to have had at least one began to enter her thinking and she sent off for a book on sex to see what she had been missing.

Armed with this determination she picked an appropriate moment to talk to her husband Keith. Keith was dumbstruck. Was Joyce now saying that their sexual relationship had been no good all of these years? Was he going to have to turn into a sexual athlete to please her? This damn class was putting silly ideas into her head.

Disappointed by his response, Joyce dropped the subject, saying – as much to convince herself as Keith – that they were all right as they were. But the thought wouldn't go away, and it became a persistent niggle at the back of her mind. Joyce remembered that at the back of her 'sex' book there was a list of addresses where help for problems could be sought. She decided to contact Relate. She saw her counsellor for the first time the day after her sixty-first birthday.

Keith and Joyce's story was not an unusual one. They had married in their early twenties, had no sex education to speak of and had had little sexual experience before marriage. Keith was slightly ahead of Joyce in that he had had intercourse once with a previous girlfriend, but Joyce was still a virgin when they married. Their courting never got further than heavy petting because Joyce was terrified she would become pregnant like her older sister, who 'had to get married'. So Keith and Joyce learned together about sex and developed a comfortable routine. It was over fairly quickly, didn't involve a lot of foreplay, was pleasing enough and could be expected to happen on Saturday nights after *Match of the Day*.

Joyce had decided that there was no point in beating about the bush with the counsellor; she would have to ask straight out if she was seen as a foolish old woman. She told the counsellor that she had come to get help because she had never had an orgasm and wanted to find out whether she was too old to have one. Reassured that it was never too late, they talked together about Joyce's experience of sex. Joyce found it surprisingly easy to talk and to take in the information she was given about a woman's sexual responses. Joyce was told she could be referred to a specially trained sexual counsellor if she wanted to take things further.

Joyce felt she needed to go home first to think through what the next move might be. It took her a week to tell Keith where she'd been and another to persuade him that it was all right for her to continue. She somehow felt it was important that he should be supportive of what she wanted to do.

Joyce returned and began work with the sex therapist. She learned a lot about where her attitudes and beliefs about sex came from. She was encouraged, in the privacy of her own bathroom, to look at herself and her sexual parts and to locate her clitoris. Initially Joyce was resistant, but as she came to understand that this self-exploration was important in giving her the information she might need to help Keith know more of what she liked, she became more comfortable.

In her teens, Joyce had missed out the phase of adolescent development associated with sexual self-stimulation. Among the strict warnings about sex Joyce and her sisters received from her mother were that you only ever touched yourself 'down there' with a flannel, you didn't wash your hair when you had a period and you 'mustn't let boys take liberties'. None of this was ever spelled out any further, but there was no doubting the underlying message: sex was dangerous and bodies were no-go areas.

Gradually, over a number of weeks, Joyce blossomed as she

gained in confidence. She still didn't like the idea of touching
and stimulating herself but she was now able to share with
Keith some of her learning. She could show him how to touch
her and what felt good. She was more than happy to let him
do so now during foreplay, which increasingly formed an
important part of their love-making. Up until now their love-
making had been little more than intercourse.

Keith read the book about sex and admitted there was a lot
in it he had not known. Joyce had her first orgasm through
Keith's touch very quickly once they got the hang of it. It was
an enormous relief, and Joyce shed tears of happiness which
were mopped up by Keith. Both of them felt they had been
given a new lease of life.

We all have a right to know the unadorned facts of life. But
facts alone will not help us to achieve what most of us want –
true intimacy with another person. Even when in possession
of the facts, mistaken ideas about male and female behaviour
lingering over from a past era can get in the way. David
and Yvonne provide an example of this. Their marriage was
characterised by continuous arguments about sex. These rows
were the only blight in an otherwise good marriage – but they
had been going on for fifteen years, and eventually drove
them, in their late fifties, to seek the help of a counsellor. The
problem seemed to be a difference in sexual appetite, as David
described it. He would try to initiate sex two or three times a
week, but Yvonne would always succeed in resisting his
advances and only 'allow it once a month'. What David found
mystifying was that when they did make love it worked for
both of them. He had never managed to get her to talk about
her apparent lack of interest in doing something that she
clearly enjoyed. He finished up calling her sexless; she told him
he was sex-mad.

The counsellor asked each of them to say how they had
learned about sex and what it meant to them to hear the
criticisms of the other. It gradually emerged that both had very
stereotyped views of the sexual natures of men and women.

Yvonne had acquired the idea that all men without exception were ready for sex at any time, and that women had a responsibility to keep them in check. For his part, David clung to the notion that all women needed a lot of persuading before they would agree to have sex and that even if they said no it was important to keep trying. If you didn't carry on in the attempt, they would shut down completely.

David and Yvonne were like a lot of couples for whom the marital bed had become a war zone for the battle of the sexes. The sexual relationship, instead of bringing loving reassurance and intimate comfort, became a power struggle, where the game was to win. For David, winning meant getting sex. For Yvonne, winning meant succeeding in withholding it. It was a pattern of relationship which was getting them nowhere fast – except closer to the divorce courts. Both of them agreed that when they did make love it was good for them both. So how to break the impasse?

David and Yvonne had to do an awful lot of talking. They found it difficult at first to listen to each other and really take in what the other was saying. But in their sessions they learned to accept that each of them had a right to their point of view and that there were two truths in any relationship.

They were helped to recognise that a positive way forward for them both would be to come to a negotiated agreement about the frequency of sex. David conceded that there was little point in pressing Yvonne for sex three times a week and actually 'getting it' once a month. Yvonne admitted that once a month wasn't enough for her either, but resisting the demand for it had become a point of principle.

The breakthrough came when they agreed to have sex once a week. David would initiate sex once a week but agreed that he would not press Yvonne for more than that. Yvonne agreed, but added that she would like to feel she could take the initiative if she wanted. This was a surprise to both of them. Both agreed to try this new way of relating, and could see that it had the potential to give them both more of what they wanted. David wanted more sex, Yvonne wanted less pressure.

By the time they returned for a follow-up appointment some weeks later, David and Yvonne were able to report that, by and large, they had stuck to their negotiated pattern (barring one incident when David, a bit the worse for wear after a party, had forgotten the agreement and had become over-amorous. Yvonne laughingly said that he didn't take much putting off and was asleep in no time!)

The new way seemed to be helping a lot. They no longer rowed over sex or sniped at each other in front of others. Friends had commented on the difference and pulled their legs saying, 'Whatever you two are on, we want some of it.' They were both relieved to be back in the bedroom and off the battlefield.

THE POWER OF THE SENSES

Our need to be touched is such a profound part of being human that it is with us from birth to death. Touch is powerful because when we exchange touch we communicate with each other at a very primitive level. Babies, who cannot speak or walk, respond wholeheartedly to touch. They start to make sense of the world through experiencing how things feel – infants test things out not by asking questions but by grasping objects in their hands and putting them in their mouths.

By the time we have reached adulthood, we have learned to speak and listen and have mastered a phenomenal range of other skills, intellectual, social and practical. Wine-tasters and perfume blenders apart, grown-ups – unlike babies – take the power of the senses more or less for granted. They become part of our day-to-day human repertoire. Unselfconsciously we exercise taste, smell, hearing, sight and touch all the time. We swallow food we like or spit out what we don't. We turn up the radio when a favourite song comes on or clap our hands over our ears at the sound of a pneumatic drill. A particular smell can instantly take us back to a past time in our lives – or tell us that something's burning in the kitchen. We plan our gardens around an appealing colour theme or rip off the previous tenant's ghastly wallpaper. We test the bathwater with our toes; we stroke the cat. All the time we make choices based on information about what is nice and what is nasty that comes from exercising our senses.

Even if we are not 100 percent conscious of it, every one of our senses plays a vital part in our enjoyment of sex. Becoming more fully aware of the interplay of the senses enriches our sexual experiences enormously. As we get older touch can become one of our most important sources of comfort, reassurance and communication. Most women know that they have always needed a lot of caressing and stroking as part of the right conditions for sexual arousal. They know that short-cutting foreplay can mean an indifferent sexual encounter. Men, on the other hand, can find themselves ready for intercourse within minutes – and as a consequence, they miss out on the rewards of sensuous touching. As a man gets older, however, he begins to need more of the foreplay his partner has always enjoyed. Couples in touch with their sensuous side understand this, and incorporate more caressing and stroking into their lovemaking to ensure that the conditions for sex are right for both of them.

What many couples start to discover is that a more sensuous kind of lovemaking is deeply rewarding in its own right. The need for penetrative sex every time becomes less important. Specialists in the treatment of sexual problems have developed a series of intimate touching exercises for couples to do at home which help develop a more sensuous and relaxing approach to sex. Like this, sex can be not only fulfilling but creative, loving and recreational.

Restoring sensations

Sometimes, when sexual relationships have become fraught, it is important to go back to basics; to a touching experience free from pressure to perform and respond. The following exercise can be used to get back in touch with the pleasurable feelings associated with intimacy that have got lost in the tensions of unsatisfactory sex. The technical term is 'sensate focus' but basically we are talking about caressing, massaging and stroking to give and receive pleasurable sensations.

Set aside an hour when you can be alone and undisturbed – take the phone off the hook, lock the door: whatever you need to do to feel you have left the world behind for a while. It is better not to choose a time when you will be too tired. The room should be pleasantly warm and somewhere you will feel comfortable with no clothes on. Create the right atmosphere with subdued lighting – perhaps some candles – and maybe play some soft music.

Both you and your partner should have a bath or shower to help you to feel fresh and relaxed. One can take his or her shower while the other begins to prepare the room. When you are both ready, decide who would like to be touched first and who would like to be the one doing the touching. Let us say that the woman is going to be touched. She should lie down on her stomach on the bed or couch while her partner concentrates on the experience of touching her.

The man now strokes and caresses his partner's body from the top of her head to the tip of her toes. He starts at her head, then moves to her neck, shoulders, insides of the arms, hands, along her back, lightly moving over her bottom, down her thighs, right down to her ankles and her toes. He should try different kinds of touching – light butterfly caresses, massage, using the palms and the backs of his hands or using his face – all the time concentrating on the experience he is giving and receiving. It may help to close his eyes to increase awareness in the other senses.

If the woman experiences anything she finds uncomfortable she should not say, 'I don't like that,' but 'I liked the previous touching better. I'm not very happy with that.' She too can concentrate on what she is experiencing and may want to tell her partner when something feels good.

After about fifteen minutes, the woman should turn on to her back so that her partner can touch her face, neck, leaving out her breasts, across her stomach, leaving out the genital area, moving down over her thighs, legs and feet and back up again to her face. Again he should take about fifteen minutes to concentrate on his experience of touching. Then it is his turn to lie down on his stomach so that his partner can experience what it is like to touch him, and the process is repeated, again leaving out the genital areas. As before, if anything makes him uncomfortable he should tell his partner in a way that is not critical but helps her to understand more about his body.

Both of you may find that you touch areas of your partner's body that you had forgotten about or that you had never been aware of before: soft bits, round bits, smooth bits, hairy bits, that evoke particular feelings. Just be aware of the feelings. Concentrate on the experience rather than getting into conversation. When each of you has had a turn at touching and being touched, just lie in each other's arms and have a cuddle, telling each other what you experienced: what you saw, what you smelled, what sounds the touching made, whether you were aware of the smell and even the taste of each other.

A few days later, you might wish to repeat the experience, but this time may want to include touching of the penis, vulva and breasts. Or you may simply want to repeat your first experience.

The most important things about 'sensate focus' are that there are no goals, no pressure and no demands – just a shared intimate experience.

Many couples get bedevilled when the expectation persists that everything will continue as it did in middle age. If we believe that, we may be disappointed. Better to be prepared and be prepared to adapt, too. So what actually might it be helpful to have in the way of sexual information? In the following chapter we offer basic facts about sexual behaviour which applies whatever your age, to which has been added information of particular relevance to people as their bodies get older.

Chapter Twelve

SEX – THE PHYSICAL FACTS

Whatever our age, we all need basic information about the physical changes that take place in our bodies during the stages of sexual experiences. We need straightforward biological information about what happens under normal circumstances and as we get on in years we need additional information on the normal changes we can expect as we get older and the effects they have.

THE MOST IMPORTANT SEXUAL ORGAN OF ALL

Without doubt the most important sexual organ of all in the human body is the brain, for not only is it ultimately responsible for the physical changes associated with sexual arousal and functioning but also for the all-important emotional and mental processes that lead to a satisfying sexual experience. It is the brain that lets you know whether the conditions for sex are right and conducive to love-making.

The brain is also responsible for producing the mechanisms that inhibit and block sexual engagement, which can impede function and lead to sexual problems. The brain registers anxiety, anger, pain, and off-putting memories and tells you to deal with these feelings first before attempting to get physically close to a partner. You can choose to ignore these signals and engage in, at best, a pretty unsatisfactory experience. If you listen to the signals and try to resolve some of the issues that are getting in the way of relating in a loving way you give yourself the best chance of improving things and getting more out of your relationship.

The brain also holds the key to many of the negative myths and attitudes that may be held about sex and sexual functioning – myths that may be propped up by poor or misleading information about human sexual behaviour.

THE MALE GENITALS

In most men the unaroused penis is about 7–10 cm (3–4 in) long. Some are smaller; some are bigger. The penis, in an unaroused state, is flaccid, soft and floppy. The tip or head of the penis is called the glans penis and corresponds to the clitoris in women. The glans penis, especially around the ridge that connects it to the shaft of the penis, is the most touch-sensitive part of the penis in most men.

The glans is covered with a skin called the foreskin. It is this skin that is removed in circumcision. When the penis is in its

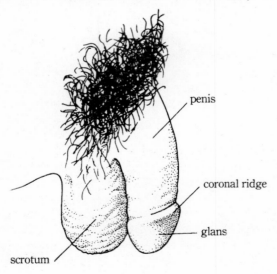

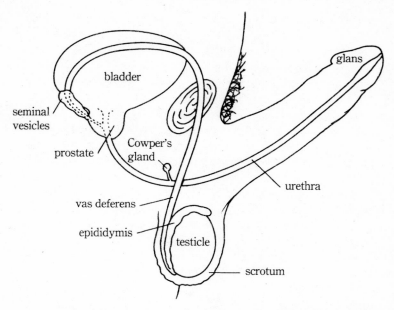

flaccid state the foreskin covers the glans except for the opening called the urethra through which urine passes. In the circumcised man, of course, this is not the case and the glans is uncovered.

The major internal sex organs in men consist of the testicles, the vas deferens, the seminal vesicles, Cowper's glands, prostate gland and urethra.

Hanging behind the unaroused penis itself is the scrotum or scrotal sac. This bag-like shape contains the two testicles and hangs slightly lower than the penis, holding the testicles away from the body. One testicle usually hangs slightly lower than the other in the sac.

Inside each testicle the production of male sperm takes place on a continuous basis. Sperm need a cooler than body temperature to be produced, which is why the testicles need to be held slightly away from the body. Sperm are stored in an area towards the top of each testicle called the epididymis until they are required in ejaculation.

Men continue to produce viable sperm throughout their lives. Although viability does reduce with age, men of eighty plus have been known to father children. The testicles are also responsible for producing the hormone testosterone.

Inside the body, leading up from each testicle, is a firm tube called the vas deferens. The vas tubes extend from the testicles to the prostate. Prior to ejaculation the sperm travel through the tubes to their upper ends to mix with the secretions of the seminal vesicles and the prostate. The secretions of the prostate contribute most of the seminal fluid or ejaculate, giving it its whitish colour and its particular odour. Sperm actually account for only a tiny fraction of the volume of ejaculated seminal fluid.

It is the two vas deferens tubes which are cut and tied off in a man who has the operation called vasectomy. The sperm can travel no further and fertilisation can no longer take place. The ejaculation of seminal fluid, however, continues as before and many men report little change in their experience of male orgasm following the operation. Sperm produced by a man who has had a vasectomy are absorbed into the body's natural elimination system.

Two small glands, called Cowper's glands, are located at the beginning of the urethra. They produce a small amount of clear, slightly sticky fluid called Cowper's fluid or pre-emission. This fluid is thought to lubricate the urethra in readiness for ejaculation and to neutralise any acid remaining from a previous passage of urine. A drop of Cowper's fluid can often be seen on the tip of the penis at the entrance to the urethra when the penis is fully aroused.

THE FEMALE GENITALS

Unlike the male genitals, female genitalia are for the most part out of sight, tucked away and covered with pubic hair. For many men and for some women they can seem somewhat mysterious. The most common proper word for this area in the female is *vulva*. Many women have never looked at their vulva and as many men may have avoided seeking to do so. The line drawing of a vulva given here is an illustration of the various parts that make up female genitals. It is the kind of view that a gynaecologist would have when examining a female patient and the view that can be had by a woman if she uses a hand mirror to look at herself.

Vulvas, like faces, are all different. All faces have two eyes, a nose and a mouth but each one is composed differently. It's the same with genitals. Just as men's genitals differ in size, colour and other characteristics so do women's; and that's normal.

The outer lips of the vulva are called the labia majora. They are usually full and fleshy and covered with pubic hair and act as a kind of protective cushion for the rest of the genitals. Inside these lips are a second, smaller set, composed of folded tissue which form the labia minora or inner lips. These inner

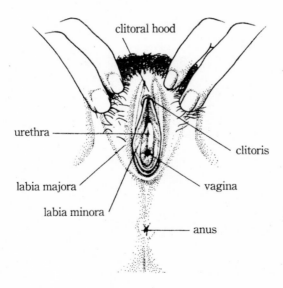

lips are often quite uneven and one side may be larger than the other. They lie closer to and surround the opening to the vagina and are usually closed over it during everyday activity. In some women the inner lips are shaped in such a way so as to protrude slightly between the outer lips; in others they are hidden by the outer lips.

In the upper area of the inner lips is the clitoris. The clitoris is a unique organ in that it has no other function than to provide pleasurable sensations. Men have nothing quite like it, for their penises are also used for urinary purposes.

The clitoris in the female and the glans penis in the male are composed of the same kind of tissue, and although the clitoris is tiny in comparison to the glans penis it has about the same number of nerve endings. It follows that it is very sensitive to stimulation. The clitoris, being so sensitive, is covered by the clitoral hood.

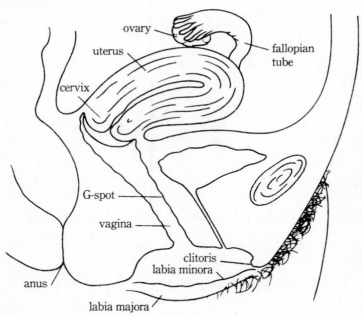

Just below the clitoral area is the opening to the urethra
through which urine is passed and directly below the urethra
is the entrance to the vagina.

The major internal sex organs in women are the vagina, the
cervix, the uterus or womb, the fallopian tubes and the ovaries.

The vagina is a potential space. The walls of the vagina lie
close together. In an unaroused state they are relaxed and
touch each other like a flattened tube. The outer third of the
vagina (the part closest to the entrance) contains most of the
nerve endings that are sensitive to touch. The inner two-thirds,
in most women, are insensitive to direct touch but may convey
a pleasurable sensation of pressure and an 'inside the body'
sort of feeling that is encountered in sexual intercourse. On the
front wall of the vagina, about 5 cm (2 in) inside, there is an
area called the Grafenberg-Spot or G-spot, named after its
discoverer, a German physician. This particularly sensitive
spot can give some women pleasure when it is stimulated.
Current evidence indicates that this G-spot appears to exist in
some women and not in others.

Inside the vagina, at the top end, is the cervix, often called
the mouth of the uterus or womb. It is completely closed apart
from a small hole which allows menstrual blood to pass. The
womb itself is the size of a small pear in a woman of childbear-
ing age. It becomes smaller, over time, in women past the
menopause.

Leading from the womb are the two fallopian tubes and
the ovaries. The ovaries carry a woman's lifetime supply
of ova or eggs. An egg (ovum) is released from one of them
each month from puberty until the onset of the menopause.
The egg is released approximately fourteen days after
menstruation starts and will find its way down the fallopian
tube and into the uterus. The uterus prepares for a fertilised
egg by thickening its lining. If an egg remains unfertilised it
will pass out of the body through the cervix and the uterus
will shed its lining through the vagina as a monthly menstrual
period.

THE HUMAN SEXUAL RESPONSE SYSTEM

It is as important to understand the human sexual response system and its apparent mysteries as it is to have accurate information about the sexual physiology of men and women. Lack of information about normal processes and functions in this area causes misunderstandings and confusions.

Basic biology is all very well but you need to know what happens when you touch here, stroke there, this response occurs, that reaction takes off. You may believe that because sex is a natural body function you should know all about it. You may believe, too, that love-making ability comes naturally and that not feeling confident about it should not be admitted, particularly when you've got a few grey hairs! By and large we pick up our understanding with experience. We serve an apprenticeship – but it can be a pretty hit-and-miss business. We can go on firing on the misinterpretation of a particular reaction in a partner for years. Far too many of us try to run our sexual relationships on the basis of telepathy. We nurture the fond hope that our partners will 'get the message' without our having to ask for what we want directly or show them what makes us feel good.

Human sexual responses are many and varied. The famous sexologist, Alfred Kinsey, said of the subject, 'There is nothing more characteristic of sexual response than the fact that it is not the same in any two individuals.' Given the variety of human sexual response, there is no right or wrong way to have a sexual experience. Each person's response is unique and the result of a complex interaction at the time of physical and emotional states, sexual stimulation and feelings about yourself and your partner. Having said that, as a guideline we offer this simple model to aid understanding and to help you to start to think about your own and your partner's particular response cycle.

There are basically four stages in the human sexual response system and they occur in both men and women:

Desire; Arousal; Orgasm; Resolution.

DESIRE

Desire, with its companion, sexual excitement, can happen in a few seconds – in response to a sexy thought or touch, the sight of an attractive person, romantic music or a stimulating film. Almost immediately, as a response, there is an increased flow of blood to the pelvic area and an increased sense of sensual awareness in the body. Pupils dilate and there is an increased awareness of the genitalia, and other erogenous parts like breasts, lips and ears. In men, the penis can begin to become erect as a consequence of this increased blood flow and for women vaginal lubrication will start to take place.

This process of engorgement (increased blood flow) can be reversed at any time by distraction, lack of further opportunity or the discontinuation of the touching. Feelings of desire can occur a number of times a day or only under special circumstances. In older men and women desire for and interest in sex is experienced but the process of increasing sexual awareness and excitement takes longer and touch becomes much more important in the creation of desire.

There are distinct advantages here for both sexes as couples recognise that they each need more foreplay and they are no longer as 'out of sync' as they may have been in the past. The 'instant' erections he used to have often generated an abbreviated period of foreplay for her, in his eagerness to get on with the performance goal of orgasm. This limited period of caresses may have left her frustrated, caught up in the same belief that only orgasm counted, yet being short-changed by it.

Women enjoy love-making most when their need for plenty of time for desire and arousal through lengthy foreplay is met. Now for both partners comes an opportunity for increased pleasure in sensual and sexual touching: a time for the man to allow himself to learn about and enjoy his sensuality in its own right rather than be dominated by some urgency to get on with the activity.

The Desire phase followed by the Arousal phase can become an important experience in its own right for many older couples, communicating as it can, the tender, loving and intimate feelings between them. The need to proceed to full sexual intercourse on every occasion of sexual contact becomes much less important as we get older and we learn to appreciate less urgent pursuits. For some the need for intercourse or orgasm as an outcome of sexual intimacy may only be one out of every three occasions. What becomes important is having opportunity for sexual expression and enjoyment rather than the goal-oriented performance of youth.

AROUSAL

When sexual desire continues into higher levels of sexual excitement, further changes occur which signal heightened sexual arousal.

In both sexes blood continues to flow into the pelvic region following continued sexual stimulation. There is an increase in breathing rate and heartbeat and the muscles of the stomach, legs and buttocks start to tense.

Male responses

In the male the spongy tissues in the penis become engorged with blood and the penis becomes larger and firmer.

In the soft state the amounts of blood flowing in and out of the penis are about equal and the penis stays about the same size. When there is sexual stimulation an increased amount of blood is pumped into the penis at the same time as the outflow is reduced. It is this pressure differential that produces the erection. The testicles are drawn up closer to the body until they press up against the wall of the pelvis. The skin of the scrotum thickens and changes texture, becoming darker in colour because of the increased blood flow. The coronal ridge around the glans penis becomes swollen and engorged and in the uncircumcised man the foreskin rolls right back, fully exposing the glans penis.

During this arousal phase it is common, particularly during prolonged love-making, for a man to lose some of the firmness of his erection. During any one episode of love-making an erection can 'wax and wane' on a number of occasions and this is normal. Provided the man does not get anxious and agitated about this his erection can be reinstated by appropriate stimulation.

Female responses

A similar process of increasing arousal is taking place in the female. The inner and outer lips become fuller and larger in response to the increased blood flow into the sexual tissues. The effect is to open up the vulval area, exposing the vaginal entrance and the clitoris. The clitoris increases in size, and is often described as being the size of a pearl. Just like penises, however, the size and shape can vary. What is common is that it becomes very sensitive to touch. The whole area darkens in colour just as the male genitalia do. Lubrication is produced in the vaginal walls in a process similar to sweating. The amount of lubrication produced varies from woman to woman and from time to time. Some women produce a lot, others only a sparse amount. The breasts and the clitoris also respond to the blood flow to the sexual areas. The breasts increase in size and in most women the nipples become erect. The clitoris, at the height of sexual excitement, retreats under the clitoral hood. Although no longer visible, the clitoris can still respond to stimulation of the area surrounding it.

During this process not only is there increased lubrication in the vagina but it has been changing in size and length. This occurs when the uterus tilts from its normal position, causing the cervix to pull on the vagina and producing a lengthening and ballooning effect near the cervix.

Like the male, the female arousal process can be reversed by similar experiences. Excitement levels drop when there is distraction or insufficient stimulation or when there is a halt in the proceedings for conversation. The reinstatement of the conditions and activities that led to the higher levels of arousal can usually restore things.

For the older couple this arousal period can be immensely pleasurable as long as they take into account a number of changes that have been occurring as part of the natural process of getting older.

For the female, for instance, there may be a reduction in the amount of vaginal lubrication produced during love-making. This can soon be rectified by introducing lubricating products like KY Jelly or Sensel, available from most chemists. Or a visit to the doctor could rectify matters with the prescription of a vaginal cream which restores some of the former glory to the vagina. These creams counteract the normal thinning of the vaginal wall that may have been occurring. It is important to recognise these changes and do something about them rather than experience discomfort or pain which can only lead, in the long term, to eventual disinclination and avoidance of sexual contact.

For the older man it's likely that it will take longer to get an erection. The penis will need more direct stimulation; just thinking sexual thoughts or kissing his partner may not be enough. But this change hasn't happened overnight. It's not as if your penis ceases to respond on your sixtieth birthday! It is likely that over time, probably since your forties, you have welcomed and valued manual or oral stimulation by your partner as part of your arousal and love-making. You would be unusual if you hadn't. Now you just need more touching, fondling and tender loving care from your partner. Your erection may not be as hard or as full as it once was but it will still be perfectly adequate for love-making. Ask your partner: you may be surprised at how much she values the slower pace, the lessening of performance pressure and the increase in loving touching that you both now do.

It really is crucially important that you both recognise that the changes taking place are perfectly normal and there is absolutely nothing that you can do to turn the clock back and prevent them. Much better to accept them. Much better to develop a wider repertoire of sexual loving than you've allowed yourselves in the past – when everything worked on automatic pilot. That very automatic pilot response may actually have limited the development and exploration of the sensual and sexual experiences now available to you both.

ORGASM

Orgasms in men and women are quite similar, the main difference being that women do not ejaculate or at least do not have the same release of ejaculatory fluid as men. In both men and women, quite simply, orgasm is a reflex response that releases muscular tension and reverses the blood flow to the pelvis region. But put like that it doesn't sound the rewarding experience it can be!

In men the experience has two phases. In the first phase, the prostate, seminal vesicles and vas deferens contract, pumping their contents into the urethra at the base of the penis; mixing the sperm with the secretions from the seminal vesicles and prostate to form the semen or ejaculate. These contractions are the beginning of ejaculation. During the second stage the muscles at the base of the penis contract rhythmically to propel the ejaculate through the urethra until it reaches the outside of the penis. This milky fluid may spurt out or it may just ooze out. Usually ejaculation is accompanied by the intense, pleasurable feelings of orgasm. The number of contractions, the amount of fluid and the force with which it leaves the penis are dependent on a number of factors, including age.

As a man gets older his ejaculatory process may take longer to achieve (there's potentially a real bonus here for lovers who like to take their time) and many men report that it's not always important every time to ejaculate. It's also likely that as a man ages, particularly past sixty, his experience of ejaculation may become less intense. This does not mean that orgasm is not pleasurable, but only that it may feel different. While the words ejaculation and orgasm are often used synonymously it may be useful to distinguish between them, for ejaculation is the physical process of propelling semen through the penis and orgasm refers to what you feel. Generally the two go together; you ejaculate and enjoy pleasurable feelings.

In women, orgasm has just one stage and it parallels the contraction stage in the male. A woman experiences, at the height of sexual arousal, the intensely pleasurable, peaking contractions in the clitoris, vulva, and vagina that form the orgasm. These rhythmic contractions may also be felt in the uterus. Orgasm or climax in sex follows no absolute pattern but almost all women require stimulation not only up to the point of orgasm but throughout the orgasm as well, unlike men who once they reach a point of inevitability, will continue to orgasm even if stimulation ceases. For most women, the interruption of stimulation just prior to the approach of an orgasm or in the midst of it, results in a very quick loss of arousal and no orgasm at all or one which is cut short. The main bonus for women when it comes to orgasms is that, unlike their male counterpart, some women, but by no means all, can have further orgasms should they so wish.

The right kind of stimulation, in the right place, is of paramount importance to orgasm in women, and here it is important to state that for many women stimulation in intercourse by the thrusting of the penis in the vagina does not do the trick. *The Hite Report* 1989, based on research with 3,500 women aged from 14 to 78, reported that only about 30 per cent of women achieved orgasms in intercourse and that most women needed manual or oral stimulation to come to climax.

Important information for all lovers

The clitoris needs sufficient direct or indirect stimulation to produce the intense responses needed for orgasm. The truth is that many women do not have 'no hands' orgasms and that's normal! The notion that there is a 'right way' to have an orgasm and that it must be with penetration, needs to bite the dust once and for all.

But, like men, women may begin to experience different orgasms as they get older. There may not be quite the same peaks of intense pleasure, or sexual arousal and intimacy may be enough. Arriving at a point where orgasm is a possibility may take more time and longer stimulation, and it may be necessary to create the conditions that will produce it.

For many older women, the need to have an orgasm may diminish altogether but it should not be assumed that the need for sexual closeness has vanished, for as we have seen, sexual relationships can have many meanings. We should all remember, whatever our age, that the major controller of our sexual response system is still the brain and it's the brain that will tell us whether we've enjoyed the experience or not.

RESOLUTION

For many couples it is this last phase that sums up the meaning of their sexual relationship and that meaning will be unique and personal to them. After love-making is over, and things are getting back to normal physically, a couple can feel at their closest, can take the opportunity to cuddle up and talk or contentedly fall asleep. It is important to understand what has happened in technical terms too, for it is also, potentially, a time when misunderstandings and misinterpretations can occur. In physical terms, this resolution phase means that there is a release of the muscular tension, created by being sexually aroused, and reversal of the blood flow that has engorged and sensitised the genital organs, called detumescence. For the man, basically, the body returns to where it was before the sexual experience started. The penis returns to its non-erect state but the rate at which this happens can vary from time to time. Sometimes the erection will go down immediately and at others, it will stay relatively firm for many minutes after ejaculation. Men, at this point, enter what is called the refractory period; a time when it is not physically possible to be re-stimulated to either erection or ejaculation. Quite simply, a man must wait a while before he can expect to be stimulated enough to produce another ejaculatory experience. He may get another erection, but won't be able to ejaculate, because 'the warehouse' in the personal production line of his epididymus is short of 'supply'. As one man put it, 'I have to wait for delivery from the production line.'

In a young man of eighteen, this can be a matter of minutes; in an older man, hours, and in a man in his later years, several days or weeks. It really shouldn't matter, if, when the 'production line' kicks into action the conditions are right and the feelings between partners are good.

During the period of resolution many men can experience feelings of lassitude and deep relaxation, and for some this often leads immediately to sleep, much to the consternation and disappointment of their partners. While clearly, for some men, this can be a convenient way of avoiding uncomfortable intimate discussions, sometimes there are occasions when sleep is just the best thing to do after sex.

Women, too, experience the same 'detumescence' after sex; the same returning to normal, when genitals return to their unaroused state and the vulva again envelops the inner labia, clitoris and vaginal opening and adopts its covering position of the female genitalia. This 'back to normal' process occurs more quickly if there has been an orgasm than if there has not. Sometimes, if there has been a very high level of arousal and no orgasm, the return to the unaroused state can take a considerable amount of time and there may be some discomfort. This pelvic pain can be relieved by masturbating to orgasm, if it is so desired.

For the woman this resolution phase may be a time when cuddles and talking are sought to continue the experience of closeness and intimacy. There may also be the need to relax and sleep. Understanding what is needed after sex is just as important as understanding what is needed during it and that applies to both sexes.

Clearly as we get older there are changes in sexual functioning. We may want sexual contact less frequently, we may not always want to have orgasms, we need to create the right conditions because we can't rely on things happening automatically as before. But no one need go into sexual exile. Sexual expression can be part of your life for as long as you live. There are no good biological reasons for sexual retirement. There are, on the other hand, a number of cultural myths that can cause older people much unnecessary misery. We shall tackle some of these in the next chapter.

Pause for thought

Think for a moment about how your sexual response system has changed over time.

What has changed for your partner?
What does he/she need more of?
Are you still in a hurry, or can you take the time?

Chapter Thirteen

MENOPAUSAL MYTHS AND PHALLIC FALLACIES

All of us, to some degree, are affected by the myths in our culture – particularly myths and beliefs about sex and sexual relationships. It is bad enough to be affected by ridiculous false notions when we are young but as we get older we are also faced with a fresh battery of sexual myths, coloured by ageism. This short chapter highlights some of the common myths that inform sexual attitudes today.

Myth 1
Old people, especially those over sixty, don't have sex.
Where does this one come from? Certainly not older people. It is mostly the young who have a hard time imagining Grandma and Grandpa having sex. Grandma should bake cakes, knit and babysit and Grandpa should sit in his rocking chair, reminiscing about the good old days to anyone willing to listen. They no longer need sex to keep them contented and loving.

What utter nonsense! Sex is just as enjoyable in older age as in youth. So why should we be expected to give it up? To save others' embarrassment or foolish discomfort? A tangle of tales has grown around late-life sexuality that is coloured by the false notion that the reservoir of sexual need dribbles away into the sand, emptying, never to be replenished, at some time between the ages of sixty and sixty-five.

But research evidence shows nothing could be further from

the truth. The American Starr-Weiner study of 800 people between the ages of sixty and ninety-one found that 95 per cent of them enjoyed sex; indeed for 75 per cent, sex was as good as it had been when they were younger, if not better than before. The desire for intimacy, the need to be physically touched and loved does not fade with age, nor should we let it. Sex is not just for the young and beautiful, simply because they have the attention of the press and broadcasting media. In fact, sex, dictated by the urgent haste of youth, may be wasted on the young. A mature wine is more rounded and full-bodied than this year's pressing.

Myth 2
Sex after a certain age isn't good for you.
When seen as a physical event of Olympic proportions, sex could rightly be described as 'a bit too much' for the over sixty-fives to participate in. But long periods of heightened heart rate and breathlessness do not form part of most people's sex lives whatever their age. A happy, regular sexual relationship with a much loved partner is good for every bit of you and rarely dangerous – unless of course you're into swinging off that chandelier!

Myth 3
All women prefer large, hard penises.
The fact of the matter is that most women are not fussed about the size of the penis. And as there is absolutely nothing that can be done to make a penis bigger than it is there is little point in worrying about it. Size is an irrelevance, it's how the penis is used that really counts. What is more important is the capacity to 'make love'.

Myth 4
You have to have an erection to have sex.
The thinking behind this myth is that sex is only sex if there is penetration and anything less is somehow second-best. What

tosh! And what pressure that places on a man to always come up with the goods.

The one thing guaranteed to frighten off erections is pressure – pressure to perform. This myth in particular makes a man very vulnerable, for he knows he can't control his penis or get an erection through force of will. He can't fake it or hide the lack of one.

Penetration is just one part of love-making and the penis is not the only sexual part of a man. The experience of loving foreplay can be deeply satisfying for both partners and certainly an erection isn't needed to bring a woman to orgasm.

The less importance a couple places on erections the better. Erections only appear when conditions are right and there is no pressure for anything in particular to happen.

Myth 5
Women's bodies cease to respond sexually as they get older.
It is true that changes in hormone production following the menopause affect vaginal lubrication with the subsequent possibility of dryness and discomfort. None of this means that women cannot continue to respond to loving caresses and foreplay and enjoy sensual stroking and touching.

At the menopause the secretion of the hormones progesterone and oestrogen gradually decreases and then stops. The loss of oestrogen, particularly, can mean that women begin to experience vaginal dryness. Lack of vaginal lubrication can be remedied by using a water-based lubricant such as Sensel or KY jelly or the application of an oestrogen-based cream in the vagina, prescribed by your GP.

Some oestrogens are produced naturally elsewhere in a woman's body, particularly in the fat of plumper women, and many women experience little change in their physical response system.

Myth 6

If you can't get an erection when you want to, it's better to give up.

Better to give up pressurising yourself to get one! It simply isn't possible to conjure up erections. They aren't something you can produce at will. Most men know that penises have minds of their own and don't behave themselves if the conditions aren't right and they are not getting what is needed. But it's certainly not sensible to give up altogether and retire from the sexual scene. One of the saddest consequences of giving up on sex is that often this can mean that all forms of physical affection are dispensed with for fear that the partner may want more than just a cuddle.

Myth 7

As you get older you lose interest in sex and can't do it any more.

It is surprising how many men and women let themselves be seduced by this myth. Like a self-fulfilling prophecy, for them it comes true. For many this disinclination and lack of interest in sex may stem from the fact that their experience of sex has never been a very fulfilling one or that their desire and drive has always been on the low side. No one is saying that sex is compulsory in old age, but finding ways to express our need to be loved and to share loving times together is an imperative for everyone.

Myth 8

After you've had a heart attack you should stop having sex.

The general rule of thumb that most doctors use is that if you can climb a flight of stairs without getting breathless, resuming sexual relations should not be a problem. If a man who has had a heart attack wants penetration in intercourse, making love with the woman in the 'on top' position is often recommended as it can maximise the eroticism and minimise the effort.

Talk to your doctor. If he or she tells you to avoid sex, seek clarification and ask for a further opinion, preferably from someone who specialises in sexual problems. Remember that your GP has, with that recommendation, consigned you to early sexual retirement and it may not actually be time for you to collect that particular pension. It's always worth seeking specialist advice.

These eight myths are in many ways the tip of the iceberg when it comes to phallic fallacies and menopausal myths. Ageist attitudes do not just exist in the young but also in ourselves as we take them on board and subscribe to them. We may be our own severest critics when it comes to our right to sexual expression, feeling that we shouldn't, mustn't, ought not to have and need sex. We may tell ourselves that we are too wrinkly, sagging, over-the-hill, grey-haired, arthritic, over-weight, respectable, too elder-statesman to want sex. Not true!

We owe it to our children and those who come after us to claim our sexuality in old age. If we don't do it, how will they?

Chapter Fourteen

SIGNS OF THE TIMES

While active involvement in sexual relations for older men can be inhibited by failure of erectile function, women's active participation in regular sexual activity can be affected by the lack of available male partners due to bereavement. Quite simply, women outlive men.

These issues notwithstanding, the two most common sexual problems encountered by older men and women are impotence and loss of or lack of arousal which leads to loss of interest. In both instances the difficulties seem to lie in the failure to respond to sexual stimulation. Just as we have seen that the physical response system in men and women is similar, it is likely that a parallel process also takes place when it comes to sexual problems.

A number of physical changes take place as we get older. Here we focus on some normal changes that may affect sexual functioning.

CHANGES EXPERIENCED BY WOMEN

Menopause

These days most women can expect one third of their life to be post-menopausal. In the last century and into the beginning of this one, the menopause could with some justice be seen as heralding not just the end of a woman's fertile years but, with an average life expectancy of not much more than fifty, the beginning of the end. Post-menopausal then meant old. Not any more. Most women reach the menopause when they are between forty-five and fifty-five – usually at about the same age as their mother and grandmother. The difference is that now women can look forward to about another thirty years of healthy life.

The idea that the menopause signals the end of women's sexually active years is losing ground in the last third of the twentieth century, when the notion of sex as a purely pro-creative activity has all but disappeared. There are a number of reasons for this change of attitude, which together have transformed our thinking about sex as recreation, not just pro-creation. Having said that, there have always been women who welcomed the menopause because it meant that they could enjoy sex with their husbands without fear of pregnancy.

Menopause simply means that monthly periods come to an end. For some women this is exactly what happens -- they just stop. But for others, periods become irregular both in frequency and in the amount of bleeding. This stage may last a few months or several years. Medically the menopause is thought to have taken place when a woman has not had a period for twelve months.

The most common symptom of menopause is hot flushes, often associated with night sweats. Neither of these occur-rences is in the least harmful or a sign of anything being wrong, but some women find them embarrassing and uncom-fortable. A hot flush usually begins with a feeling of slight pressure in the head, followed by a wave of heat passing over the body. A blush spreads over the face and neck and some-times there are tingling sensations in the body. Night sweats are often extreme enough to wake the sleeper (and the person lying next to her!) as she throws off the covers and finds she has to change into clean, dry nightwear. Reduced levels of oestrogen are responsible for these symptoms too, and three out of four women experience them. For most women, episodes like this fade away in the course of two or three years. Some are not so lucky and have to put up with them for much longer.

Short or long term, you may prefer to avoid stressful or exciting situations which might trigger a hot flush. Calm, deep breathing during a hot flush makes it easier to cope with, rather than getting into a flap and making it worse. It's also useful to dress in lots of thin layers so that the top one – a jacket or cardigan – can easily be slipped off when you need to cool down.

Night sweats can, not surprisingly, disturb sleep patterns, and many women going through the menopause report suffering from insomnia. In its turn, lack of sleep can cause irritability during the day. This would be the case for anyone of any age, man or woman. It is useful to remember this as it can be easy for people to blame the menopause for all sorts of 'symptoms' that are just a normal part of life.

Once the menopause is complete, it is not possible to become pregnant, but because the menopause takes place over a period of time rather than suddenly, it is wise to take contraceptive precautions until the menopause is complete. The most suitable contraceptives at this stage are 'mechanical' methods such as the condom for men and the diaphragm for women. The contraceptive pill and the intra-uterine device are not recommended for menopausal women.

All the changes associated with the menopause take place because of changes in hormone levels: a fall in oestrogen, an absence of progesterone and a rise in pituitary hormones. Because the level of oestrogen in the body is fluctuating during the process of menopause, variations in bleeding occur. Sudden surges of oestrogen cause heavy bleeding, for example. Oestrogen is the hormone which stimulates the womb to prepare itself for pregnancy once a month and has other important functions. It is most active on the tissues of the breasts and genitals, which is why as time passes and the levels of oestrogen decrease, women experience changes in the breasts and vagina. These changes happen gradually and are not exactly the same for every woman. Having said that, by the age of about sixty-five most women will notice that their breasts are flatter and less firm than they used to be, with smaller nipples. What happens in the vagina is that the lining wall becomes thinner and more easily irritated. Not surprisingly, sexual intercourse can be uncomfortable or even rather painful when this happens. Vaginitis is the term used to describe soreness in the vagina. The simplest remedy is to use a water-based vaginal lubricant to assist intercourse. Substances such as petroleum jelly or baby oil are unsuitable for internal lubrication because they can affect the pH balance of the vagina, leading to thrush or other infections. They can also affect the strength of condoms. Water-based products such as KY Jelly or Sensel can be applied by hand either to the vagina or – and this works better – to the man's penis. Using a lubricant can add to the sensuous pleasures of foreplay and become an enjoyable part of love-making.

Your doctor can prescribe a vaginal cream containing hormones which will improve the condition of the vagina itself. For Shirley, aged fifty-seven, this was the ideal solution. She had always enjoyed a happy sexual relationship with her husband, Paul, until she arrived at the menopause. Over the space of about six months she became less and less inclined to make love because it always seemed to hurt. She simply was not lubricating as she had before, so intercourse was almost always rather painful.

When she first went to see her family doctor about the effect the menopause was having, he wasn't terribly helpful. He told her she was well over the worst symptoms and that if she was patient things would improve. Shirley had decided she did not want to take hormone replacement therapy and in talking to the doctor about her intimate life had played down the pain she was experiencing during sex. But continuing her sexual relationship with Paul meant a lot to Shirley, and eventually she talked about what was really happening with a close female friend of her own age. As it turned out her friend had been diagnosed as having vaginitis.

Knowing about this condition gave Shirley the confidence to

go back to her doctor and say what she believed to be the problem. This time the doctor gave her a prescription for a vaginal cream which Shirley started to use straight away. Once again, sexual intercourse became something to look forward to as part of her loving relationship with Paul.

In itself, the menopause does not necessarily bring about depression, irritability or any other psychological problems. Nevertheless many women do find that at this time of hormonal turbulence they are prone to emotional ups and downs. Every woman's experience is different. Some will be determined to go through the whole thing without a blip and will succeed. Others, equally determined, will find tiredness and irregular heavy periods are almost more than they can cope with, especially if they unexpectedly find themselves saddened by the end of their fertile years. Women who face the menopause prepared for the worst might actually make it worse, by becoming over-anxious about every minor symptom. Keeping in good general health is important – the better your physical condition, the brighter your mental state is likely to be. There is further advice on this subject in the next chapter.

The most important thing for women and their partners to bear in mind about the menopause is that it is natural and normal. It is not the beginning of the end, but an important milestone in a woman's life which can mark the beginning of a fascinating new chapter. In the vast majority of cases, any problems that crop up are temporary and can either be alleviated by simple remedies or be managed by women themselves – especially if their partners are sympathetic and well-informed. If a woman is not getting reliable information and good advice from the health professionals responsible for her care, her physical and emotional difficulties are likely to be increased. Support from her family is just as valuable, and women need the men in their lives to understand the facts about the menopause and to discard the myths.

Some men may feel that the menopause is 'women's business' and that there is no need for them to be informed about it. But it is insensitive not to try to understand what is going on at a meaningful stage in a woman's life. Knowing what happens during the menopause makes it easier for men to be supportive at a time when their partners might well need some reassurance.

Hysterectomy

Hysterectomy is an operation to remove the uterus or womb. It sometimes also involves the removal of the cervix and ovaries. Removal of the ovaries is properly known as an oophorectomy. One of the most common circumstances for the prescription of hormone replacement therapy is when a woman has had a hysterectomy and oophorectomy, because when the ovaries have gone the body's chief source of oestrogen has disappeared. This is especially so if the woman undergoes the operation before she reaches the menopause. The incidence of hysterectomy in older women is high, and the operation may be performed for a number of reasons, including cancer, endometreosis (inflammation of the womb) or fibroids. Some health advisers believe that hysterectomy is carried out too often – that there are some cases where treatment other than radical surgery would remedy the problem. Any woman whose doctor suggests that she should have a hysterectomy should satisfy herself that it is the best solution to her problem before going ahead.

A period of convalescence is recommended after hysterectomy as it is after any major surgical procedure, during which the patient should have adequate rest and a healthy diet. The period for physical recovery is on average six weeks, sometimes more, during which it will not be advisable to lift even moderate weights or to drive. After that, and all being well at the post-operative check, life can go back to normal – including the resumption of sexual intercourse. Be that as it may, for a number of women things are rather different; sex feels somewhat different; sexual responses are not exactly as they were before. Women who retain their cervix seem to have a better experience of sex post-hysterectomy than those who do not. There may be a need to redefine 'normal'.

Some women feel saddened by the loss of their reproductive organs. Others feel anxious that they have lost their femininity. With these concerns added to the stress put on the body by an operation, it follows that the support of a loving partner is of paramount importance in regaining self-esteem and re-establishing sexual activity. There is no physical or organic reason why your sexual relationship should not be fully rewarding after a hysterectomy, but if you are finding it difficult for any reason, ask your GP for help or to refer you to a Relate psychosexual therapist.

Osteoporosis

One of the most distressing post-menopausal symptoms which used to affect far more women in former times than it does today is osteoporosis. Commonly known as 'brittle bone disease', osteoporosis is disabling and painful. The bones in the body inevitably get thinner with the passing years, regardless of gender. By the age of ninety, however, one in three women and one in six men will have suffered a fracture of the hip because of this process. The figure for women is higher because of the drop in the level of oestrogen and other sex hormones. The classic symptom of osteoporosis is a crumbling of the spinal vertebrae, producing a decrease in height and curvature of the spine (which at its most pronounced is the condition known as 'dowager's hump'). When a pregnant woman or breastfeeding mother is told to increase the calcium in her diet, it is not just to protect her teeth, but to prevent bone loss, too. Poor diet is likely to be to blame for the suffering of women of our grandmothers' generation. Clearly preventive measures are essential. These include eating a diet with adequate calcium, taking enough load-bearing exercise (like walking) and giving up smoking. Women who have been smokers, who have had the eating disorder anorexia nervosa or who have been over-athletic to the point of ceasing to menstruate are at higher risk of contracting the disease. What has also been discovered is that bone loss in women after the menopause can be considerably reduced by hormone replacement therapy.

Hormone Replacement Therapy (HRT)

Hormone replacement therapy does exactly what is says on the packet – it gives back levels of the hormone oestrogen which the ovaries are no longer producing. Women who have had a hysterectomy are prescribed oestrogen-only HRT, but women who still have a womb are given the hormone progestogen as well for part of the monthly cycle. This is as a protection against cancer of the lining of the womb (endometrial cancer), as it causes the lining to shed in a way that results in bleeding very like a period.

Your GP or health professional at a well-woman clinic will advise you which is the best type for you, should you decide to take HRT. Oestrogen comes in tablet form and in patches of small clear pieces of adhesive cellophane that are stuck to a convenient part of the body – usually the thigh or buttock. Progestogen comes as small tablets. HRT tablets are packaged in separate blister packs so that you can keep track of the days on which you are supposed to take them. Other types of HRT formulae include gels, creams and pessaries.

There is evidence that HRT not only relieves some of the physical discomforts of the menopause but also offers protection against heart disease and Alzheimer's disease as well as osteoporosis. Nevertheless, many women are unwilling to take medication for a physiological process which they regard as natural.

There is as yet little evidence that HRT has any direct effect on sex drive. It is more likely that those women who find that taking HRT relieves some of the debilitating effects of the menopause feel generally so much better that their zest for life – and the sexual side of their life – returns.

Memory

There is a school of thought which links decline in memory with falling oestrogen levels. Since the levels of oestrogen in men are low throughout life, this theory would suggest that they are always afflicted with poor powers of recollection (and some women whose birthdays are frequently forgotten would say that this is indeed so). But the most recent findings of gerontologists (scientists of ageing) show that those whose memories decline the fastest are not just getting older, but suffering from ailments such as cardiovascular disease or diabetes, and what sex you are has nothing to do with it. This isn't to say that while a woman is going through the hormonal ups and downs of menopause while coping with children leaving home or getting married and possibly the demands of an ageing parent, she will not at times leave something off the shopping list.

Everyone – male and female alike – is subject to some weakening of the powers of memory as they grow older. It varies from person to person. Tricks to enhance the memory work whatever your age, and there is good evidence that keeping your hand in mentally – with crossword puzzles, for example, playing card games and learning poems by heart – really do help. And never underestimate the value of a good list, especially if you keep it pinned to a highly visible board in the kitchen.

Stress incontinence

Many women, especially women who have had children, experience involuntary leaking of a small amount of urine when they cough, laugh or sneeze. It is not usually enough to warrant wearing special protection but it will make underwear wet. It is an uncomfortable nuisance and one that many women find embarrassing. It happens because muscle tone has been lost in pregnancy and childbirth and further weakened by decreasing levels of oestrogen. After having a baby all women are told how to do pelvic floor exercises – as Ellie (see page 48) did. Her mother Monica's experience is very common – not only in suffering from stress incontinence, but not doing anything about it until it started to affect her sexual relationship with her husband. If there are other symptoms such as burning when you go to the loo or an urge to pass water yet an inability to do so, then you should see your doctor in case there is some kind of infection of the urinary tract.

For simple stress incontinence, however, the remedy is to strengthen the weakened muscles by doing Kegel exercises for the pelvic floor at least twenty times a day – more if you can manage it. The exercises are easy to do and of real benefit to both men and women. For men, regular practice strengthens the muscles that surround the penis and improves the circulation of blood in the pelvis, a factor of obvious importance since increased blood flow to the penis is what makes an erection. Relate sex therapists recommend to all clients that they do these.

PELVIC FLOOR EXERCISES

Both men and women will benefit from regularly carrying out an exercise designed to strengthen the muscles of the pelvic floor. This exercise was developed by a gynaecologist, Dr Arnold Kegel, for women who suffered from stress incontinence after childbirth, and is known as Kegel's exercise. Many of his female patients reported greater sexual enjoyment as a result of doing the exercise and experienced stronger and more pleasurable orgasms. The benefits to men were discovered by the sexologist Bernie Zilbergeld, who having tried Kegel's exercises himself, asked some of his professional colleagues to do them as well. The results were positive and the exercises were henceforth recommended, with successful results, to men in order to increase control of ejaculation, improve erections and contribute to heightened sexual pleasure generally. The increased pleasure reported by both men and women can be attributed to the increased blood flow to the pelvic area as a result of the exercise. The exercise is extremely simple. First it is necessary to identify your pelvic muscles. The next time you go to the loo to pass water, try to stop the flow in mid-stream. To do that you have to use the pelvic floor muscles. Do it every time you urinate over the next couple of days to make sure you have identified the feeling that you need to have when doing the exercise. Once you have mastered this, you can start to squeeze and release the muscles at other times.

Start by squeezing and releasing the muscles fifteen times – just squeeze and let go. Do one set of fifteen twice a day. At first, you may also be squeezing your stomach and thigh muscles. It will take a few days until you are co-ordinated enough to squeeze only the pelvic muscles. When you have reached this point, you can do the exercise unobtrusively anywhere – watching television, waiting for the bus, reading a book.

Do Kegel's exercises every day, gradually increasing the number until you are doing around seventy twice a day. Build up slowly. When you are able to do that number comfortably, you can also do a slight variation. Instead of immediately releasing the contraction, hold it for a count of three, then relax and repeat.

You can do both the long and short variations, making two sets of each every day, or alternate between them – doing the long one day and the short the next. Continue doing both for at least six weeks. You will have to wait for a month or more for the results to be noticeable, but as you continue to do them they will become automatic and require no conscious attention or effort.

Women can use the exercise at any time during sexual

activity to enhance arousal. Each woman is different in how her body responds – just relax and enjoy the feeling. A man who has mastered the exercise can use it to develop ejaculatory control either by relaxing the muscles when he feels close to orgasm or tightening the same muscles as he nears ejaculation. Both variations work, but it may take a little experimentation to work out the precise timing by paying attention to the feelings of sexual excitement.

It is a good idea to take other forms of exercise that improve the blood flow to the pelvic area such as swimming, and, as luck would have it, sex.

CHANGES EXPERIENCED BY MEN

Lessening of strength

For women, menopause signifies a milestone in life which usually occurs at about the age of fifty. Men have no equivalent experience. But as men get older, certain physical changes gradually occur. Very broadly, these changes could be described as a gradual lessening of strength. These changes vary from person to person according to genetic make-up, general health and well-being and personal circumstances. They are not dramatic. Perhaps it takes a little longer to swim the usual twenty lengths; instead of lifting a heavy piece of furniture single-handed, another pair of hands is needed; digging over the vegetable patch leaves the keen gardener a little short of breath. Most men take these changes in their stride. Similar changes affect men's sexuality; and in this area of life some men find it more difficult to be philosophical.

Erectile failure

For men, the most distressing sexual problem is what used to be known as impotence and is now generally referred to as erectile dysfunction. This is the expression used to describe any situation in which a man is unable to get an erection. It is not uncommon – in fact it is estimated that one in ten men in the UK aged over twenty-one suffers from the problem at some time. A man who has never had an erection is said to have 'primary' erectile dysfunction. 'Secondary' erectile dysfunction is when a man who has usually been able to achieve an erection without any problem suddenly finds that he cannot do so.

A number of causes of erectile dysfunction can be treated successfully. Impotence can be a great blow to a man's self-confidence. He may also feel that he has 'failed' his partner whom he loves. He may feel ashamed and not know how to seek help. But help is available and much can be done, particularly if the problem is treated in the context of the relationship and with the support of his partner.

The causes of erectile dysfunction can be divided broadly into two categories, physical and psychological. Physical causes include conditions which damage the nerves or blood vessels that supply the penis, such as diabetes, high blood pressure, furring up of the arteries, such as occurs when the man has high cholesterol levels, and spinal injuries.

The nerves and blood vessels can also be damaged as a result of surgery on the rectum, prostate gland and bladder or by radiotherapy to the pelvic organs in the treatment of cancer. Another important physical cause of impotence is drugs. Many, but not all, drugs prescribed to treat high blood pressure and various drugs used for psychiatric conditions impair erections. Only rarely is impotence caused by hormone problems such as having too little testosterone, the male sex hormone.

The most common psychological cause of erectile problems is fear of failure. The man becomes so preoccupied with the thought that he will not get or keep his erection that he can't relax enough to respond during sex. Other common causes are associated with tiredness, worry, depression, guilt and the late twentieth-century disease, stress and fatigue.

Changes in men's sexual response do not usually become evident until past the age of fifty, but at any time from forty onwards, less frequent desire for sex begins to be evident. It may take longer for the penis to become erect. Over time, there seems to be less emphasis on ejaculation itself. The sensation experienced during ejaculation changes, and when it is over, the older man finds that his penis loses firmness very quickly after orgasm. It may take longer than it used to to have another erection.

As they become aware of these changes taking place, some men become concerned about what they see as a loss of virility. In the back of his mind, a man has an idea of what it is to be a man: to be a generous provider, for example, to be successful at work, to do well at sport, to be a good lover. He worries if he thinks that he is not performing as well as he might in any of these functions. He becomes anxious that he is losing his sexual ability, and his self-confidence suffers.

Harry first experienced failure to get an erection shortly after he was made redundant at fifty-five. He had thought that his job was safe and would not be affected by a recent takeover. One morning, however, he was called in to see his boss and told of the changes: his job was gone. He was asked to clear his desk by lunchtime.

Several weeks later, Harry was still 'in shock'. He got a decent redundancy package but was very traumatised by the experience. Not surprisingly he began to have erection problems – his penis was also becoming redundant. His wife Joan was very understanding, but as Harry became more and more worried, sex became a pretty miserable business.

Harry had never had problems with sex before. He'd always been ready for sex at a moment's notice, day or night. He became convinced that there was something wrong with him, and although humiliated by having to ask for help he eventually went to his GP and was referred to a urologist.

It was a long, anxious wait for the first appointment. Harry had a thorough examination and a number of tests and nothing amiss was found. He was referred back to his GP and was told that all he needed to do was stop worrying and relax. Easier said than done, for Harry had lost all confidence in his ability to keep an erection. He would sometimes wake up with an erection in the morning but the minute he started to think about using it he became anxious about whether it would stay hard enough for long enough. And like a self-fulfilling prophecy, he found himself becoming limp again.

Harry's problem was psychological rather than physical. The cure lay in regaining his confidence in his wayward penis. Harry, with Joan, was referred again by the GP, but this time to Relate's psychosexual therapy service. After several meetings where full sexual histories were taken and some of the reasons for the difficulties explained, Harry and Joan began to make more sense of why they had been visited with the problem.

Harry and Joan knew that in some way the redundancy and the erection failure were linked. The fact that sex had always worked for them hadn't given them a chance to develop the skills they needed when it didn't. Harry, a bit of a natural worrier anyway, had been catapulted into anxiety about everything when he became redundant. He began to observe his own performance as a lover, as if he were outside his body looking down on his penis, willing it to work.

At home, Harry and Joan embarked upon a programme of touching exercises that helped them to re-establish their sexual relationship. To their surprise, the first thing the therapist did was to put a total ban on any attempts at intercourse. Harry took a bit of persuading, but eventually was convinced that, as trying to have intercourse was a constant reminder that he couldn't do it, it would reduce his anxiety about his performance if he stopped trying.

The first exercise involved Harry and Joan going back to first principles and agreeing to set aside specific times when they would retreat to the privacy of their bedroom and take turns to touch and massage each other sensuously. They could

fondle and caress the upper body and legs, but in no circumstances were they to touch each other's genitals. They were
encouraged to tell each other what they liked and what they
were enjoying but essentially they were simply to engage in
an intimate time without any pressures. At first they were
embarrassed and awkward, wondering how on earth it could
help, but in the event, and encouraged by the therapist, they
were surprised how nice it felt to be physically close again
without all the anxiety.

The second exercise was a repeat of the first, except that
fondling each other's genitals could now be included, although
only as part of the general touching and not for arousal.

At their regular meetings with their therapist Joan and
Harry talked about how they had got on, and were given
advice as to what to do next. Both of them commented on how
relaxing they had found their touching sessions. Harry had
actually had an erection on two occasions, but Joan had
insisted they should not break the ban.

As the weeks passed, they progressed to touching which
aroused Harry to erection and then was stopped for a while
to allow the erection to subside. Joan was very patient and
loving and was instructed to arouse her husband to an
erection two or three times in any one touching session.
Gradually Harry gained in confidence that his erections could
come and go and would not be lost for ever. He felt back
in control. Better still, he had become much more in tune
with Joan's need for specific ways of being touched sexually
in their love-making as he learned to fondle and caress
her body in the sessions. Harry liked the new lover he was
becoming.

The ban on intercourse was lifted. Harry and Joan were
recommended to proceed to intercourse with Joan on top,
whenever it felt right in their love-making session. The woman
on top position is easiest at this point. Joan was to be in charge
of the proceedings and Harry was instructed to let her put his
penis into her vagina and not worry. Of course, at the first

attempt Harry got anxious and lost his erection within seconds but Joan, not to be daunted, simply withdrew his penis and re-stimulated it as she had learnt to do. The erection was restored – along with Harry's confidence – and they had intercourse for the first time in eighteen months.

Harry announced to the therapist at their next meeting that he thought he was 'cured'. As a bit of insurance, Harry and Joan asked to meet with their therapist twice more, but in fact they didn't really need the extra sessions. The last appointment was cancelled because Harry had been shortlisted for a job for which he was well qualified with a firm who had a reputation for taking on older, experienced men. A second phone call brought the news that he had got the job. The following day's post brought a thank-you letter which the therapist still treasures.

Harry and Joan and gained a lot from working together on the sexual problem. It had brought them closer together. They had gained new skills which would stand them in good stead to manage the ups and downs which are normal in a long-term sexual relationship. The mutual trust, effort and loving they shared and showed all contributed to resolving the problem.

The story of Ben illustrates the way in which a man's confidence in himself can be hard hit when he feels that his sexual performance is not as good as it should be. Ben worked in the health service as an administrator and retired at sixty-five. His wife Mary was sixty-three. They came together to see a Relate sex therapist about six months after she had had a hysterectomy. Ben had began to experience episodes of erectile failure – in other words, he had not been able to achieve an erection when making love to Mary.

There was more to the story than that, however. Mary had always seemed to be the strong one in their long and successful marriage, and when they learned that she needed surgery, Ben was devastated. He felt that he just couldn't cope if she became an invalid. He worried about it constantly. One evening when he was due to give a speech at the local Rotary Club, where he had just been given office, he completely lost his nerve and had to sit down after only a few minutes. As someone who had often had to speak in public during his working life, this lapse was totally out of character. He began to be afraid to go to the club meetings.

In fact Mary recovered from surgery very well. There was, however, a difference in the way she felt during love-making. Penetrative sex, which had always been an important part of their love life, was now less satisfying than it used to be, and Ben was aware of it. With his background in the health service he had known just which books to consult and had done a lot of reading not only about erectile failure but also about the causes of anxiety attacks and how to treat them. After he had failed to get an erection several times, and shortly after the incident at the club, he told Mary he had decided to seek professional help. She was very willing to join him at a consultation with a sex therapist.

The therapist took a detailed history from Ben and Mary. It became clear that since there had not been any incidence of erectile failure in the past, since both were in good health and in a relationship that was important to both of them, the chances of a successful outcome to therapy were high. Ben wanted to make love to Mary in a way that would give her pleasure, as he had always done. In their love-making of earlier years foreplay had been a relatively brief prelude to penetrative sex. Now they learned to bring foreplay into the foreground. They learned to relax, spending as much time as they liked on touching and stroking each other, kissing and whispering sweet nothings while Ben brought Mary to climax by stimulating her with his hands. It was a revelation. Mary was able to have orgasms again. Ben was delighted and as his anxiety ebbed away, so his self-confidence and his erections returned. Their sex life was richer and more varied than it had ever been. Needless to say, Ben carried on in his role at the Rotary Club with no more problems.

__WHEN THINGS DON'T ALWAYS WORK __

All sexual relationships go through ups and downs, the peaks and troughs of everyday life. When things are happy and relaxed between you sex is likely to be good and much more on the agenda unless you have other difficulties. When couples are under stress or not getting on with each other sex is bound to suffer and it can get pretty 'frosty' in the bedroom.

One of the first and most important things to say, however (and most sex therapists would hold to this) is that you can't have sexual problems on your own! If your wife now has problems having an orgasm then it's likely that you will feel affected by this; if your husband finds he has started to ejaculate very quickly and things are over in minutes you may feel a bit shortchanged on the action.

The second important thing to know is that not always functioning sexually in a way that you might wish is absolutely normal. No one functions 100 per cent sexually, 100 per cent of the time. There are times when the earth is expected to move and it doesn't. And there are times when you find yourself disconnected from the love-making and thinking 'we must get this ceiling painted' or 'I wish I hadn't started this 'cos I'll never get up in the morning.'

The time to seek help is when problems persist. Help in understanding and resolving the difficulties is available. Here we seek to outline some of the more common sexual problems experienced by men and women in later life and their possible causes, and we identify some of the appropriate treatments that are available.

Lifestyle and erectile dysfunction

We are all pretty well informed about some basic rules of health. For example, we know that eating lots of sugary foods leads to tooth decay and that exposure to the sun's rays can cause skin cancer. Cigarettes have health warnings printed on the packet and we are always being told to keep our alcohol intake within limits. Sometimes the connection between these useful pieces of advice and the consequences of not heeding them is brought uncomfortably close to home. There is now clear medical evidence that smoking and drinking can seriously affect the cardiovascular system. Vera and Ron are a case in point.

Vera came to Relate to see if she could do anything to help her husband Ron to get his erections back. She had read an article in a magazine at the hairdresser's about treatment for sexual problems and had torn it out to take home to Ron. The article had recommended going to Relate. Ron read the article and said there was no way he was going to see anyone. Vera could go if she wanted. So she did.

Ron had had problems for a number of years and because they were now in their sixties, they believed that nothing could be done. They still had sex 'of a sort', as Vera put it, but both missed being able to have intercourse and if there was any chance of improving things, Vera wanted to take it.

Ron hated being impotent. It had come on gradually in the past five years. To start with his penis just didn't feel the same and now it wasn't working at all.

Vera came home from her first meeting with the therapist full of enthusiasm and determination for Ron to attend and get help. She had made an appointment for them both for the following week and there was no way Ron wasn't going to be there – he knew that when Vera got that look on her face there was no stopping her. If he didn't do what she wanted there'd be hell for weeks – but all the same it was a reluctant Ron who turned up with Vera for the appointment.

Vera did a lot of the talking at the beginning, explaining how things had been and how they were now. Gradually, Ron was drawn into the conversation and began to feel more confident that some help might be available. He had expected to feel embarrassed, but instead he felt 'This guy understands'. The therapist, Paul, explained that he would need to do a full assessment and would need to see them a number of times. Ron would need to see his GP to have a medical check-up to make sure that there was nothing organically wrong, such as diabetes, high/low blood pressure, the effect of certain medications and cardiovascular disease.

During these early meetings it became obvious that Ron and Vera had a very supportive relationship. They had been together for a long time and, as Ron put it, 'I love the bones of her and I always have.' What also emerged was that Ron and Vera were both life-long smokers, and that Ron had had a couple of very large whiskies every night for the last twenty-five years. All this had taken its toll on his vascular system and was thought by his GP to be underpinning Ron's failure to get erections. The doctor recommended that they stop smoking straight away and cut down the drinking.

Ron and Vera felt as if they had been asked to climb Everest but agreed to try. Paul felt they might welcome a brief therapy programme of touching exercises done at home together. They agreed, and although over the weeks they enjoyed touching and massaging each other, there was no sign of a return of an erection. Paul decided to lend Ron and Vera a video of a pump which can be used to produce an erection. The pump works on a vacuum principle and gives an erection which is firm enough for intercourse.

Home they went with the video. Ron sent off for the vacuum pump and a month later they brought it with them to their session with Paul. Vera told of the hilarious time they had had when they first tried it out, but – miracle of miracles – they had got the hang of it and Ron had got an erection. It didn't feel quite the same as before but for the first time in years they had 'proper sex' and that was what was important to them. Vera said Ron wasn't to worry because it felt the same to her!

Ron and Vera had found their solution. Using the vacuum pump restored something that they had missed in their lives. Both of them managed to reduce their smoking and Ron cut down on the whisky. They very soon recovered the cost of their new toy.

Prostate problems

In men over fifty, the prostate gland often becomes enlarged, and inhibits the flow of urine. The prostate gland lies just below the bladder. The urethra, which carries urine out of the body, goes through the middle of the gland. The most common symptom of an enlarged prostate is the need to get up in the night several times to pass urine. The amount passed is smaller than usual and sometimes afterwards there is a feeling that the bladder has not been emptied. In severe cases it can be extremely difficult to urinate. Sometimes an enlarged prostate can make it painful to have an erection.

In mild cases of enlarged prostate it helps to empty the bladder frequently, not letting it become too full. All men with enlarged prostates should watch their alcohol consumption, as an excessive intake will make the symptoms worse. Men who experience difficulty urinating should as a sensible precaution consult their GP for a routine examination. Long-term severe cases of enlarged prostate are occasionally dealt with by an operation to ease the pressure.

COMMON PROBLEMS

Aches and pains

Two of the commonest complaints among older people are rheumatism and arthritis, labels which include a whole range of conditions affecting the muscles and joints. As we get older, almost everyone, male and female, experiences some level of stiffness in the muscles and joints, which may cause pain or discomfort and limit activity. Back pain in particular, from which huge numbers of people suffer, can make it difficult to enjoy sex.

People who are overweight are at increased risk of muscular pain, because of the extra strain their system is under. This is one of many reasons why we should try to keep our weight down. If regular, sensible exercise is part of your lifestyle, this will help in the battle of the bulge as well as keeping you supple. Swimming and walking are excellent forms of exercise with many benefits.

Treatment for the usual run of aches and pains usually consists of rest, pain-killing drugs such as aspirin and the application of heat, for example from a hot water bottle. Constant low-level pain is very tiring. Add that to back pain and the effect on your sex life can be depressing. But there are solutions. The relaxation exercises described on pages 239–242 are good for relieving stress, which contributes to back pain, and will get you in the mood for a sensuous massage. Give yourself plenty of time and make sure the room is comfortably warm.

Try out different 'low-stress' positions for sex until you find what is most comfortable. Here are some ideas. If either partner is flat on his or her back, a small cushion or rolled-up towel in the small of the back or under the neck can give useful support. The woman can go on top if her husband has back pain.

If both have back pain, a useful position is as follows: the woman lies on her back, a cushion under her back if it helps, with her partner facing her, lying on his side. She bends her legs enough for him to bring his legs forward, underneath hers. She can then rest her legs over his. He can now control the position of his back during intercourse, she is relaxed and they are in a face-to-face position.

Or, the woman lies on her side, and the man lies on his side facing her back so that he can approach her from behind. She can turn slightly to face him or roll forward if it is more comfortable.

It can be very relaxing to make love in a semi-reclining sitting position. The woman sits on a chair or couch and slides her hips to the edge – maybe with a pillow to support the lower back. Her partner kneels in front of her on the floor, his knees on a soft surface. She can raise her knees towards her chest during intercourse or rest her feet on the floor.

Alternatively, the man sits on an armless chair and his partner sits on his lap, either face to face or with her back to him, whichever is more comfortable.

The woman can kneel beside a bed or sofa, leaning on its flat surface, so that her partner can kneel behind her and enter her from behind. Both will need pillows or cushions underneath their knees and can adjust them to the right height.

Men who find the traditional 'man on top' position uncomfortable could try a variation in which the woman lies on her back with pillows beneath her lower back and buttocks so that she is raised up enough for him to kneel between her legs. She can keep her legs bent or stretch them out, whichever feels best.

Use your imagination and try different positions. With luck there will be several that you find suitable and you will have introduced some fun and variety into the bedroom. If a certain position causes discomfort, don't immediately feel you have to give up attempts at love-making. Take a rest and when you can, try something else.

Cardiovascular problems

The term cardiovascular is used to describe the body systems that include heart function and circulation. Among cardiovascular diseases are hypertension (high blood pressure) and angina. People with these problems will have narrowing of the arteries in varying degrees – possibly as a result of long-term smoking, a poor (that is, high-fat) diet and a sedentary lifestyle. Any impairment of the circulatory system will have an impact on sexual function. If you have read Chapter Twelve on physical facts you will understand that an efficient blood supply is necessary in order to achieve the levels of arousal that produce male erection and female lubrication and engorgement.

A complicating factor with high blood pressure is that some of the medication commonly prescribed to deal with the condition interferes with erectile function. Men who are placed on a regime of medication for hypertension should check with their doctor what the likely side-effects will be and discuss with the doctor what can be done to minimise them. Women, too, may be affected in the same way and should consider the same approach to their GP.

Diabetes

When a man has an erection the blood vessels in his penis fill up with blood and make it hard. Diabetes can cause damage to small blood vessels and to nerves, making it more difficult both to become aroused and to respond to arousal. A complication of diabetes is hardening of the larger arteries, which can also affect the blood supply to the penis. In fact a man who goes to see his doctor because of impotence will be checked for general circulation problems, to make sure he is not in danger of heart disease or stroke.

The research into the effect of diabetes on female sexuality is less advanced but it seems likely that women will be affected in the same way as men. As women are still physically capable of having sex, diabetic women may not be presenting symptoms for treatment in the obvious way men do and may not be being diagnosed.

Diabetes may have the effect of weakening the erection but the man might be so worried about this that he fails to have an erection at all. Anxiety and concern about his relationship need attention as much as the physical cause of impotence. Treating the impotence alone without taking into account the context of the man's life is to look at only half the problem, as the story of David shows.

David had been a diabetic for a long time when he met Jessie. He had been living alone since his marriage of fifteen years' duration ended. There had been two relationships in this ten-year period that had petered out because they just hadn't felt right. Neither of the women he had become involved with had been able to accept the fact that, so far as David was concerned, his children would come first until they no longer needed him. He also knew that he had been something of a disappointment as a lover because of his diabetes.

Now, aged sixty-two, David had found Jessie. His children were long grown and starting families of their own. It felt right to start again with a new partner, but despite his best efforts, he could not have intercourse. David told the Relate sex therapist at his first interview that it had been at least seven years 'since the damn thing worked'.

David was a loving and generous man. He was keen to satisfy and please Jessie even though he couldn't get erections. Their love-making was never rushed and he loved the intimate touching they did. Jessie said that she was happy. David, however, harboured the fear that in the end she would lose interest if they could not have intercourse, as his previous partners had done. It was this concern that had prompted David to seek advice from Relate. In discussion with his therapist David was able to talk through his options and was recommended to seek a referral through his doctor to a urologist specialising in the treatment of erectile dysfunction.

Eventually David got his appointment. After a number of tests he was given an injection of prostaglandin into his penis. This was no big deal for David, who had been self-injecting insulin for his diabetes since he was thirty-four. Fifteen minutes later David had the hardest erection he had had in years, and was of course over the moon with the treatment. He was prescribed Caverjet, a relatively new treatment, given instructions for its use by a specialist nurse and sent home a happy man. See page 221 for further information about injection therapy.

Naturally he expected Jessie to share his delight in his new-found potency, and at first she did. But increasingly Jessie indicated that she was less than enthusiastic about his injecting his penis. She felt that his physical responses had nothing to do with her and their love-making – and he had to inject himself enough anyway. David was dismayed that Jessie seemed to want to go back to how it had been, preferring their loving relationship as it was.

Driven by disappointment, this time they both sought out the therapist David had seen before. In their sessions together they talked about their attitudes and feelings about penetrative sex and its place in their loving relationship. Jessie realised that David needed this option in his life. David realised that Jessie loved him for his loving ways – not just for his penis. Therapy helped them to explore ways in which the Caverjet injection could be incorporated into their love-making should they so wish, rather than David going off to inject himself in the bathroom. Most importantly, they learned that they did not always need to progress to intercourse to have a really satisfying and loving relationship. Having the option was important, but penetrative sex was not the be-all and end-all for them.

Heart problems

Research into the sex lives of people who have suffered heart attacks seems to indicate that while for men who have problems the principal difficulty is to do with sexual arousal (in particular achieving an erection), with women it is sexual desire that is most likely to be affected. The findings of medical research always need to be set in context, of course, and one of the reasons why anyone who has had a heart attack might hesitate to resume a normal sex life is fear that they might precipitate another attack. A good rule of thumb, given the go-ahead from your GP, is that if you can climb a flight of stairs without becoming breathless, then having sex should not be a problem. Paula and Bob are a good example of a couple who may have settled for a sexless life but for the intervention of a helpful GP.

Paula and Bob were in their mid-fifties when their sexual relationship ceased. Bob was an accountant working in a big firm and Paula ran the local National Trust gift shop. Both were keen gardeners and were in the middle of enthusiastically creating a water garden when Bob got the first pains in his chest. They went off after a while and he put them down to wind. Later that day, after supper, he had a heart attack which put him in hospital for ten days. It was a terrible shock to both of them. Bob had almost died. He was put on beta-blockers and was off work for another two months. He was told to avoid stress and 'overdoing it' – and not a lot else. He was given some leaflets on diet and exercise but no advice about resuming his sexual relationship. It wasn't a question he could ask without being embarrassed or, worse still, misinterpreted as sex-mad!

In Bob and Paula's minds, having sex was one of the things Bob needed to avoid. Sex equalled 'overdoing it', so they had to give it up. Over the months, both accepted this but separately mourned the loss of something that had been a source of pleasure and comfort. Something precious was lost to them. They still cuddled and were affectionate but didn't let things go too far for fear of causing the dreaded stress.

Two years after his heart attack Bob went for his regular check-up. This time he saw the new GP in the practice. In addition to routine questions she asked him how he was getting on with his medication and whether he'd experienced any problems in his sex life. Bob was quite taken aback. More than that, he was surprised to hear that he was expected to have a sex life at all! The new doctor first explained that sometimes the drugs prescribed for heart conditions could have a dampening effect on a man's erections and in those circumstances a change of drug may be necessary.

Bob uncomfortably told the doctor that he hadn't tried having sex since his heart attack, although he still wanted to and regularly woke up with an erection. It took only a few moments for his GP to reassure him that, provided he could climb a flight of stairs without difficulty, resuming his sex life was entirely in order. She suggested that he should think about 'getting back in business' and if there were problems with erections she would consider changing his medication.

Leaving the surgery, Bob was now faced with a new problem – how to tell Paula? In the end it wasn't that difficult. What was more difficult was getting started again after a two-year gap. After some initial hesitation on both their parts they found themselves, cautiously at first, resuming their loving relationship, allowing the cuddles to develop into foreplay and manual orgasm and then taking the plunge and finally having intercourse. Bob and Paula were happily 'back in business'. Friends noticed the difference and asked what they were taking that made them look younger. 'Lots of sex,' said Bob – and they thought he was joking.

When men seek medical solutions to sexual difficulties, they may be given whatever is required to put a physical problem right without any reference to their partner. But all sexual encounters involve another person. It can be tremendously helpful for the partner to learn, as Jessie did, how the treatment can be incorporated into their usual love-making. The fact that this isn't always the case may explain why a large number of men who start off using a sexual aid optimistically have given it up altogether within a year. If a sexual problem exists, it affects two people, and both need to be involved in dealing with it.

By not looking at the sexual relationship as a whole, but by focusing on – for example – the man's difficulty in getting an erection, the idea is perpetuated that the only good sex is high-octane performance sex. The many and various delights of a loving relationship are pushed to one side in the pursuit of one part of it.

Loss of interest and desire

In the early days of sex therapy, not being interested in sex was a complaint that was exclusively female. Although loss of desire is still mainly presented in therapy by women, men are now presenting this difficulty in increasing numbers, including young men.

In later life loss of interest in or desire for sex can occur in both sexes. Loss of *desire* needs to be separated out from loss of *sex drive*. Men and women can still experience drive without desire; they may be aware that they have sexual feelings and thoughts but not in connection with their partner.

Loss of desire can occur for many reasons – as a result of illness, pain and discomfort, depression or because of attitudes which veto sex after a certain age. Absence of desire based on psychological rationales such as, 'I don't fancy him/her now' or, 'I'm not getting much out of it' or, 'At my age I really can't be bothered' need to be thought of in the total context of the relationship rather than simply being seen as sexual problems.

It is quite normal not to feel desire for your partner all the time, particularly when you have been lovers for years and everything is more than a bit familiar. It is somewhat unrealistic to expect sex always to be passionate and overwhelming or even that your partner will always be able to send you wild with desire! On the other hand if love-making has become routine, boring and unsatisfying it would be quite natural to feel 'off' sex.

If the trouble is that your lack of desire for sex is more connected to a difference in sexual appetite between you – your husband wants more sex than you and you feel pursued (as in the case of Hughie and his wife) then the feelings associated with sexual contact can turn into anger, guaranteeing further loss of desire and interest.

Depression is a great killer of desire, too. If you are feeling depressed don't expect to feel sexual. Your interest will return when the depression lifts. Medication can also affect desire. Some prescribed drugs have side effects which inhibit desire. Talk to your GP. Your loss of interest may be nothing to do with your relationship with your partner.

Whatever the cause, an open conversation between you and you partner about how it feels for you is essential and can go a long way towards dispelling the feelings of rejection he or she may have.

Difficulties with orgasm and ejaculation

Ejaculatory control, often a problem for younger men, seems to come automatically with ageing. The fact that you are no longer likely to be 'quick on the trigger' is usually regarded as a bit of a bonus. But orgasm can begin to take longer to reach and the desire to ejaculate every time tends to diminish with age – and that's normal.

Ejaculation can be experienced as less powerful, particularly in men over sixty and semen may seep out of the end of the penis rather than be expelled out under pressure. This does not mean that orgasm is not pleasurable, it is just somewhat different.

Like her male counterpart a woman may experience a diminished need for orgasm or may find she takes longer to arouse and come to climax. The orgasm too may feel less intense on occasion. As orgasms vary so much in quality and nature and can be different from one love-making to another this is not usually a cause for concern, as long as the sexual experience as a whole is a satisfying one.

Pain on intercourse

Both men and women can experience pain on intercourse, and it is always wise to have this checked out by a doctor. Technically, this pain is known as dyspareunia. Pain in the penis usually has an organic cause. In women, pain can be caused by pelvic or vaginal infections like thrush. Sometimes the pain on intercourse can be caused simply by there being insufficient lubrication in the vagina when penetration is attempted. The woman is allowing intercourse to take place when she is insufficiently aroused. In older women, even when feeling aroused, a post-menopausal condition called vaginitis (dry vagina) can commonly occur and this will produce pain on penetration. Effective treatment with hormonal cream prescribed by your GP usually rectifies things.

Surgery and sex

Radical surgery can have a significant effect on our perceptions of our bodies and our acceptability as sexual partners. Ileostomy, colostomy, radical treatment for cancer, pelvic surgery, mastectomy, surgery for prolapse and hysterectomy, all of these treatments and many others leave us in shock and having to re-think our lives. Recovering from surgery takes time. Some surgical procedures will affect sexual function, others will affect our image of ourselves as sexual people. Adjustment and renegotiating what is possible are the key factors in returning to a loving physical relationship. How you re-design your post-operative sexual relationship is up to you both, but do not forget that the closeness brought about by intimate touch can be a vital and health-giving aspect of loving in later life. Early sexual retirement may not be the best thing.

Good sexual health

If sexual activity among older people is largely unacknowledged, then so is the idea that older people are vulnerable to sexually transmitted diseases. In fact a lot of older people never think about this issue themselves. There is some justice in this, since the prevalence of sexually transmitted diseases (STDs) is highest by far among people aged between sixteen and twenty-four. Furthermore, it is known that couples who have only ever had one partner are extremely unlikely to contract any kind of sexually transmitted disease, assuming that they are in good general health and observe the usual rules of hygiene. Be that as it may, men and women who are sexually active and who have more than one partner are vulnerable to STDs, no matter what their age is. The occurrence of sexually transmitted diseases among the over-fifties is already of concern in the USA, where the high divorce rate (and, so it is thought, the availability of Viagra) have doubled the number of people in that age group contracting HIV (human immunodeficiency virus, which causes AIDS).

While there is a high proportion of stability in couple relationships between older people, there are situations in which it makes sense to take extra care. If one partner has just one affair in the course of a long marriage, for example, there is a possibility that the third party has had other lovers. Two older people forming a relationship in later life, whether hetero-sexual, gay or lesbian, might expect that their new partner has had sexual relationships in the past. No matter what their ages, couples who for one reason or another have to spend periods of time apart – for work reasons, or because of travelling – may be put in situations where they are tempted to 'have a fling'. It is not unknown for someone who spends extended periods of time in two different locations to have steady partners in both. In all these situations the chances of infection are increased.

Anyone who is in a sexual relationship other than with a long-term constantly faithful partner should practise safer sex. What that means is always using a condom for penetrative sex. Once you've got used to them, condoms are not the passion killers some people believe, and putting one on can be incorporated into love-making. Safer sex is the responsibility of both partners, in the same way as the pleasure of sex should be shared. Sex without penetration – kissing, stroking, sensuous massage and masturbation – is pleasurable and safe.

The most common symptoms of sexually transmitted diseases for women are a change in the normal discharge from the vagina, which may become itchy and sore; a stinging feeling when passing water; a rash, sores or warts around the vagina, or pain when having sex. Men may also experience a burning sensation when passing water, a discharge from the end of the penis or a rash, sores or warts on or around the penis and testicles. There could be many reasons for such symptoms, and it is important to seek medical advice. Many of these problems are easy to treat. It is possible to carry a STD with- out knowing it. In particular, people who carry HIV might not show any signs of the disease until up to ten years after infection.

If you think it is possible that you or your partner may have come into contact with a sexually transmitted disease, it makes good practical sense to have a check-up at a clinic specialising in their treatment. In a sense, that is the easy part. The difficult part, for many people, is actually talking to each other about it. This is particularly the case where one partner has had an affair. The partner who has felt they have suffered betrayal may be forgiving and the marriage or relationship may continue. But the situation after the affair is fragile, and he or she may not want to test their trust in the other so far as to suggest that they should pay a visit to the clinic. Talking about hurt feelings and repairing broken bridges is hard enough. And yet making sure that you are in good sexual health is as important a part of starting again as being in good emotional health. The staff at sexual health clinics are practical, friendly and completely non-judgemental. They are there to help.

Self-examination

At the age of fifty women are offered a mammogram, which is a type of X-ray aimed at discovering any abnormalities in the breast tissue which may indicate the early signs of cancer. Usually women will be called back for further mammograms on a three-yearly basis. All adult women should get into the habit of examining their own breasts on a monthly basis to look for lumps and for any changes in appearance, such as puckering of the nipples. Start by standing in front of a mirror and simply look at your breasts. Lift first one arm then the other to check for puckering of the skin and to check the underarm area. Feel all around each breast with the fingers. Now lie down on the bed and again feel all around each breast with your fingers. If you find a lump, go to your doctor and ask to have it checked. By no means all breast lumps are malignant; some are just water-filled cysts. But all should be checked as soon as possible and the sooner any necessary action is taken the better.

All adult men should examine their testicles on a monthly basis to look for lumps and any abnormalities. The signs to look for are hard lumps on the front or side of the testicle; swelling or enlargement, whether or not there is discomfort or pain; or an unusual difference between the testicles. If any of these symptoms are present, or if there is a heavy or dragging feeling in the groin, you should see your doctor and ask for a medical examination.

By examining yourself on a regular basis, you will become familiar with your body and be able to spot any changes quickly. If you are unsure about self-examination, make an appointment at your local well-woman or well-man clinic and ask to be shown what to do. You will also be given a thorough check-up and have the opportunity to discuss ways in which you might improve areas of your life such as diet.

HELP FOR THE PROBLEMS

Many of the couples talked about in this book have illustrated the complex nature of human relationships and just how easy it is to be at cross (in more than one sense!) purposes when it comes to sorting out tensions and problems that occur in the cut and thrust of living together as couples. If the problems that lie at the heart of your sexual relationship are located in your feelings and interaction as a couple then you need the help of a sex counsellor and therapist. Sometimes what is needed to get the best results is a combined approach: medical help and sexual therapy.

Sex and relationship counselling and therapy

Sex therapy and relationship counselling are always recommended when unhappiness with the relationship seems to colour or affect the sexual interaction that takes place between the partners. Couples and individuals can be helped to explore and resolve their anxieties and concerns about their sexual relationship and the current consequences for the sexual activity between them. Once a thorough assessment has been made, a treatment regime can be specially designed for the unique sexual difficulties presented. Some set tasks can be carried out at home. These exercises help to understand sexual needs, to diminish performance anxiety and to encourage more positive communication between you.

Relate therapists recognise that sexual problems are difficult to talk about and are specially trained to put you at your ease. There are regular meetings with the therapist over a number of weeks and most couples are amazed at how much they learn to enjoy being with each other in a less demanding, loving way.

Medical treatments

While recent years have seen major improvements and developments in the medical treatment of male sexual problems, research into female sexual dysfunction is much less advanced and as a consequence it is not possible to offer information on the treatment of female disorders. Research into female subjects has almost exclusively concentrated on reproductive problems rather than sexual function.

Alongside a range of help available to treat organically based male erectile dysfunction is an increasing emphasis on the need to combine medical and psychological therapies to ensure the most effective and long-term successful outcome for the patient and his partner.

Treatment for erectile dysfunction

Oral treatment: Sildenafil, more commonly known as Viagra, is a drug which can be taken by mouth and is very effective for many men in restoring erectile function. A small tablet is taken one hour before sexual activity is anticipated.

Unlike other drug therapies, sildenafil only produces erections if the penis is sexually stimulated in foreplay or sexual self-stimulation in masturbation.

The manufacturers claim high success rates but also report that there are dose-related side effects in some men such as headache, dyspepsia and changes in colour vision. Viagra is not recommended for anyone who is taking any form of nitrate therapy or has recently had a stroke or heart attack.

A recent Department of Health ruling about the treatment of erectile dysfunction in the NHS has restricted the treatment to a very limited category of patients. Treatments are, however, being made available through private clinics.

Intercavernosal injection therapy: Intercavernosal injection therapy involves injecting a drug called alprostadil directly into the spongy bodies on the side of the penis. The drug facilitates increased blood flow into the penis and an erection usually occurs within ten minutes or so whether or not there is sexual stimulation. Side effects include penile pain, reported in 37 per cent of users, and for some men, prolonged erections (priapism) which can cause damage to the body of the penis. All users are given instructions as to what to do in the event of this happening. Fibrosis and bruising may also occur at injection sites after repeated use.

Initial injections are given under medical supervision and the patient is taught to self-administer his injections. Good success rates are reported in people who are well-motivated but the treatment is not the one of choice for many men and their partners as it is experienced as invasive. If the injection therapy can be incorporated into love play by the couple there is an increased chance of continuing successful use.

Intraurethral therapy: This therapy involves introducing a narrow pellet, with the trade name MUSE, into the urethra at the tip of the penis. A small applicator is used to administer the drug which dissolves rapidly and produces increased blood flow into the penis which promotes erection. Erection is normally achieved within five to ten minutes and lasts for about thirty minutes to one hour. The disadvantages of this treatment are penile pain, reported by 30 per cent of users, and burning sensations in the penis for some minutes after insertion. A small proportion of female partners report vaginal burning and itching. This treatment is experienced by some patients as less invasive than others.

Vacuum devices: The three main components of a vacuum restriction device are an open-ended cylinder into which the penis is inserted, a vacuum pump that is operated by hand or battery and a constriction ring. The operation of the vacuum device begins with the placing of the penis into the cylinder and pumping to produce a vacuum. This is done for a number of minutes. The vacuum pulls blood into the penis and the constriction ring is slipped onto the base of the penis and the cylinder is removed. The erection produced is sufficiently rigid to allow penetration. The constriction ring must be removed after thirty minutes because of the risk of damage to the penis. Side effects are generally minor but the penis can feel cold and the sensation of ejaculation can be impaired. The vacuum device is suitable for most men who experience erectile dysfunction although its cumbersome nature, with the accompanying lack of spontaneity, may not be accceptable to many couples. It can also be quite expensive, but maintenance costs are minimal.

Surgical treatment: Surgical treatment for erectile dysfunction is, for most men, a last resort, after other treatment options have failed or are contraindicated. The surgery involves opening up the penis and inserting either a semi-rigid rod or an inflatable implant. There is a high incidence of complications with this treatment, as can be imagined, but it does offer some men a solution when all else has failed.

Chapter Fifteen

FIT FOR LIFE

'If I'd known I was going to live this long, I'd have taken better care of myself' is a famous remark that has been attributed to W.C. Fields, among others. But it doesn't really matter who said it, since the message is very much to the point. A useful postscript might be: 'It doesn't matter how long you've lived, it's still worth starting to take care of yourself.'

Thousands of people are obsessed with jogging, aerobics, doing circuits at the gym as if an Olympic level of fitness to keep the body beautiful is the be-all and end-all. But bodies are primarily for living in, not for looking at. We should look after our bodies well enough to enable us, the thinking, feeling people inside them, to live the life we want. The better we feel, the more we can enjoy life and our relationships.

To be physically healthy you shouldn't smoke, you should drink alcohol only in moderation, take sensible amounts of exercise, get enough rest, eat sensibly, and keep yourself clean.

To be completely healthy you also need to be in good shape mentally and emotionally – which means being adaptable, good-humoured and stable, or 'happy in your own skin'. This means knowing how to manage stress, being free from depression, being sociable and interested in what's going on in the world.

You may say to those you love, 'Take care of yourself.' It speaks of affection and concern. But you may need to learn that it is not selfish to give affection to yourself, too. Two well-cared-for people have a lot more to offer each other than a couple who are always tired, or always going down with a cold, or too overweight to get out and about – or stay in and make love.

YOU ARE WHAT YOU EAT

It's true. A person whose diet is deficient in the essential nutrients will suffer from a range of problems. Some deficiencies reveal themselves fairly quicky and obviously. A serious lack of vitamin C, for example, will reveal itself as a nasty skin ailment called scurvy while at the same time weakening the immune system. Shortages of the B complex vitamins make people irritable and unsettled as the nervous system is starved of the nutrients it needs to function efficiently.

Every so often some miracle food or food supplement is hailed as the answer to warding off the ageing process. The truth is that there is no single factor (certainly no wonder substance) which is responsible for a long and healthy life – rather it is a combination of nature and nurture; nature meaning our genes and other biological factors; nurture meaning our physical environment, the kind of society we live in, and whether or not we are getting enough good food to eat. There is nothing miraculous about the beneficial effects of eating sensible quantities of a variety of healthy, tasty foods. That is what is meant by a balanced diet, and it doesn't take a rocket scientist to work out what it consists of.

The first thing most people think of when they hear the word 'diet' is losing weight. But simply being slim is not an indicator of fitness, and it is just as unhealthy to be too thin as it is to be seriously overweight. What you need in later life is to maintain a sensible weight, neither skinny nor too fat. In practice this may mean reducing calorie intake, even if you have never had much of a weight problem, because as you get older you need fewer calories. It follows that if you carry on eating the same amount as you always have without being active enough to use up the calories, you will gain weight.

No one finds rolls of fat or distended beer bellies attractive in themselves or others. Whatever the aesthetics, however, carrying an excessive amount of weight is a health hazard because it makes people susceptible to diabetes, hypertension (high blood pressure) and arthritis. There is evidence to show that obesity affects life expectancy. After the menopause, women store excess weight differently. Instead of gaining weight on the breasts, hips and thighs, the extra goes on the tummy – where overweight always reveals itself in men whatever their age. This body shape is associated with an increased risk of heart disease.

Drastic weight-reducing diets are not a good idea at any time of life. There is a danger that by cutting right down on calories you will cut down on nutrients and make yourself vulnerable to infection. Some older people find that their appetite is much smaller than it used to be and they too are in danger of missing out on essential nourishment. The key is to establish a healthy eating pattern at a pace that you can cope with so that eventually it becomes second nature.

Aim for balance in the diet: this means including food which provides the five essential nutrients – carbohydrates, protein, fats, plus vitamins and minerals. Fibre is also important in aiding digestion. What follows is not an exhaustive dietary guide, but aims to give some signposts to healthier eating. Books which give fuller information about food and health are listed on page 255.

Carbohydrates are an important source of energy. They can be found in sugary foods like jam and biscuits and in starchy foods like potatoes, bread and rice. Starchy foods are a good source of carbohydrate because they make you feel full, contain varying amounts of protein, vitamins and minerals and are good for the digestive system. Generally speaking they are relatively inexpensive. Sugary foods are bad for the teeth, sometimes (as in biscuits) include unhealthy levels of fat and rarely (except fruit jams) provide any vitamins. But they taste nice and give pleasure – so don't give them up completely: just ration yourself. Cut out the sugar you won't miss too much – using a sweetener in coffee, for example – so that you can have a slice of chocolate cake with your Sunday tea.

Throughout life the tissues in our bodies are being broken down and need to be replaced. This is the vital function of *protein*. We are inclined to think that protein means meat, but in fact it is found in a whole range of foods, including bread and vegetables. We only need 40 g (1^1/2 oz) of protein a day to maintain health. Having said that, you would have to eat nearly 400 g (1 lb) of bread or 200 g (7 oz) of meat to obtain that level. It is much more appetising to get our protein from a variety of interesting sources, such as meat, fish, fruit, vegetables and cereals. This is what you get if you had a meal consisting of lean meat or fish with potatoes, carrots and broccoli followed by rice pudding and stewed fruit.

Fats and oils are the most concentrated form of energy food. They are classified as either saturated or unsaturated. Saturated fats are usually solid and, with the exception of palm oil and coconut oil, are derived from animal sources. They contain cholesterol, the waxy substance which lines the walls of the arteries and contributes to coronary heart disease. Unsaturated fats are usually liquid oils made from vegetables, nuts or seeds. Neither mono-unsaturated (for example, olive oil) nor polyunsaturated fats (for example, corn oil) contain cholesterol. Polyunsaturated fats are thought actively to keep the cholesterol level down.

A low-fat diet is healthy; a no-fat diet is not, because we need a certain amount of digestible, preferably unsaturated fat for energy and to make food palatable and easy to chew and swallow. The vitamins A, D, E and K are found at their highest concentrations in the fatty parts of food.

There has been a great deal of research into the effect of fat in the diet on heart disease. Some of what we read is confusing and appears to be contradictory. New findings are being revealed all the time. What has been generally agreed, however, is that fats should not make up more than 35 per cent of your food intake, and what fat you do eat should be of the unsaturated variety. A bit of thought is required to meet this target, because there is so much 'invisible' fat in foods, especially convenience foods; and often foods labelled 'low-fat' turn out to be high in sugar. Sausages and pork pies have much more fat than skinless chicken breasts or poached fillets of plaice: if you like such things, eat them in moderate quantities, and not very often.

Cheese is delicious and an excellent source of calcium (see below), but it is high in fat and calories. As little as 30 g (1 oz) of cheddar cheese provides 207 mg of calcium – more than a quarter of the daily requirement for an adult woman – and about 100 calories. For cooking, half-fat cheese is perfectly acceptable. Skimmed and semi-skimmed milk is higher in calcium than full-fat milk but far lower in calories and fat. Because milk includes levels of all the vitamins and minerals needed for good health it is an important source of nourishment for people whose appetite is depressed, perhaps when recovering from a bout of 'flu.

> The recommended daily requirement of calories for a man over fifty is about 2,400. For a woman over fifty, it is about 1,800. If you are leading a sedentary life, you might need less. If you are a fairly active person, you may need more.

Certain fish oils are positively good for you because they are rich in omega-3 fatty acids, that appear to offer some protection against heart disease and stroke. The Japanese, whose diet is very high in fish, are the most long-lived race in the developed world. Oily fish are salmon, mackerel, sardines, tuna and herring – both fresh and canned varieties of all of these are very good for you.

Fats eaten without carbohydrates are difficult to digest and may make you feel nauseous or give you a headache. The custom of eating bread with butter, crispbread with cheese or pasta with olive oil has a sound scientific basis!

Vitamins were not known to exist before twentieth-century scientists identified them, using the now-familiar alphabetic system to tell them apart. All the vitamins are essential and none of them can do the work of any other in regulating the normal functioning of the body. Nor can the body produce the vitamins for itself – they have to come from the food you eat. If you are eating a balanced diet and getting enough food, you probably do not need to supplement your food intake with vitamin pills. Having said that, there is some evidence that an increased intake of vitamin E (200 mg a day) and vitamin C (not more than 4 g a day) supports the immune function in older people.

Vitamin E is in wholewheat bread, roasted peanuts, cheese and milk and canned mackerel, among other foods. Vitamin C is found in most fruits and vegetables, the fresher the better (frozen vegetables have high levels of vitamin C too). Particularly good sources are citrus fruits, peppers (capsicums), leafy green vegetables, parsley and blackcurrants. We all need to increase the amount of fresh vegetables and fruit in our diet. A good rule of thumb is to eat at least five portions of fruit and vegetables every day. A cautionary note about spinach: while it does contain vitamin C and iron, it also has a tendency to draw on the calcium and iron stored in the body – so don't overdo it. (The iron in spinach is unusable – it simply passes through the body.)

People who do not get out in the fresh air enough may suffer from a deficiency of vitamin D. As this vitamin contributes to the formation of healthy bones, it is important in later life to help guard against osteoporosis. Vitamin D is found in oily fish, butter, milk and cheese.

Minerals help to build bones and teeth and help the body to release energy. They are lost through sweating, crying, urinating and defecating, so we must constantly replace them. The most important of the twenty or more essential minerals are calcium and iron. Selenium is thought to interact to good effect with vitamin E in strengthening the body's defences, but is only needed in tiny amounts. Insufficient iron in the diet causes anaemia, which will make you feel tired and light-headed. Insomnia, headaches and chest pains are common symptoms. If you suspect you might be anaemic your doctor will do a blood test to check the levels of haemoglobin and will prescribe iron in tablet form. Digestible iron is in meat (especially liver), eggs, dried fruit, potatoes and cabbage.

Calcium is of particular value as we grow older. It is vital for the formation of bones, and it is never too late (or too early) to make sure that you are getting enough of it. Lack of calcium makes the bones weak and porous, and osteoporosis is the result. As the production of the hormone oestrogen drops at the time of the menopause, the danger of osteoporosis increases because oestrogen is essential for the build-up of calcium deposits. Women are therefore much more prone to osteoporosis than men; but men are not invulnerable. The recommended daily intake for adults is 700 mg a day, but the National Osteoporosis Society recommends that women over forty-five take in 1500 mg of calcium a day (reduced to 1000 mg if they are having hormone replacement therapy), and 1200 mg for women over sixty-five. Many food products these days are calcium-enriched – look at the labels on yogurts and cereal bars. Not surprisingly, calcium is present in bottled mineral water, though the quantities differ from source to source. Typically you would have to drink half a litre to get 50 mg. A pint of semi-skimmed milk has 230 mg; 185 g (6 oz) of baked beans has 80 mg; two slices of bread (which is often enriched with calcium) has 60 mg; and 60 g (2 oz) of sardines 220 mg. Tablets combining vitamin D with calcium are commonly available.

Sodium is an important mineral present in salt, and therefore in all foods to which salt is added during preparation. Too much salt, though harmless for some people, may in others lead to high blood pressure. Most of us get plenty of salt in the food we eat and should try to eat less of it.

Fibre has no nutritional value but it provides essential

'roughage' in the diet, which helps to prevent constipation and protects against illnesses of the colon. A bowl of bran-based or wholemeal breakfast cereal is a good way of ensuring you get some fibre every day. When you peel an apple or leave the skin of a baked potato you are denying yourself useful fibre.

Your granny, with her bottles of 'tonic wine' knew a thing or two: one of the most welcome health findings of recent years is that wine, particularly red wine, really is good for you. Other kinds of alcohol, taken in moderation, are also beneficial. Water is wonderful: aim to drink two litres a day. Keep a flask in the fridge and have a glass every time you fancy a cold drink instead of a can of something sweet and fizzy.

Why bother? Some of the most common and most serious health problems of later life are associated with unhealthy eating patterns. Some of these problems can have a direct effect on how we function as one half of a couple. For example, in a certain number of cases erectile dysfunction can be ascribed to long-term excessive consumption of alcohol; or to medication for high blood pressure aggravated by high cholesterol levels; or to pernicious anaemia caused by a lack of vitamin B12. By eating and drinking sensibly we are taking responsibility for our bodies, not just to prevent ill health but to enjoy the positive good health which will enable us to make the most of our lives.

There is no shortage of information about what sort of food we should be eating and how much of it (see the booklist at the end). Sometimes, however, the difficulty lies in actually changing long-established customs – not only eating habits, but shopping and cooking habits, too. It is much easier to make a change for the better if you do it with the support of your partner. If you have reached a point in life when you have more time available, there will no longer be any excuse for buying lots of convenience foods. Once in a while it might be fun to have a take-away or a ready-prepared meal – but if you start to see planning and preparing delicious meals as another enjoyable way of spending time together, there will be more rewards than just the tasty food on your plate. Instead of TV dinners eaten in silence at the end of an exhausting day, meals can be a social event with time for leisurely conversation.

GIVING UP SMOKING

Everyone knows smoking is harmful. More people in Britain die every year from smoking-related heart disease than of lung cancer. As well as being the cause of serious and fatal diseases, it affects sexual activity because of the effect on the circulation of the blood. It is never too late to give up, but the first step is making the decision to do so and really meaning it. The second step is deciding when to do it. For some people, 'When I go on holiday', or 'When I retire', or 'On my next birthday' will work; for others, it has to be, 'Today is my last smoking day' and they stop there and then. You will know what sort of temperament you have and what will give you the greatest chance of success. Most attempts to give up gradually seem to fail – it has to be a complete stop. Tell your friends and family that this is what you are doing, and enlist their support.

Aversion therapy can help. If you decide that No Smoking Day is going to be on the first day of next month, save all your cigarette stubs from now on in a screw-top jar. Whenever you are tempted to light up, unscrew the jar and take a long, deep sniff. If that doesn't put you off . . .

As soon as you stop, the harmful processes that have begun inside your body begin to be reversed. Immediately, more oxygen enters the bloodstream and the risk of incurring lung cancer, bronchitis and heart disease decrease progressively. There is no doubt it will take resolve, and some days will be worse than others. But it is worth it.

POETRY IN MOTION

The second important piece of the healthy jigsaw puzzle is exercise. Jane Fonda was probably wrong when she coined the immortal phrase 'No pain, no gain' – exercise doesn't have to hurt. In fact the more fun it is the more likely you are to do it again and reap further physical benefits such as strength, suppleness and stamina. Exercise is good for you at any time of life. It keeps you in good shape, literally.

For women in later life there is a direct relationship between bone density and the amount of load-bearing exercise taken. In other words, if you run up and down the stairs several times a day, you will be helping to protect yourself from osteoporosis (worth remembering if you are considering moving into a bungalow). Even after the menopause, bones can still be strengthened to resist the waning levels of oestrogen by exercise such as jogging or running on the treadmill if you go to a gym; or by going for a brisk walk – better on pavements than soft grass – every day. Since older men are also susceptible to osteoporosis, this advice applies to them too. So go for a walk together!

As well as improving bone density, walking improves co-ordination and flexibility. A well-co-ordinated, supple person is less likely to fall over – but if they do, will be better able to protect themselves. Being supple means that you can perform a wide range of movements with ease – getting in and out of bed, the bath, a car; getting dressed and undressed. Keeping supple means that you ward off the stiffness and awkwardness that can plague older people and stop them taking an active part in life.

One of the best forms of exercise to improve suppleness is yoga. The principles of yoga were laid down thousands of years ago in India, where yoga is a whole philosophy of life. It can be practised by young children and the elderly and everyone in between, male and female, and as long as you are in good general health you can start at any age. Find a good teacher who will help you to learn the basic positions and sequences of movement. As well as stretching the body and improving posture, yoga promotes a peaceful state of mind. It is a powerful, natural way of dealing with the effects of harmful stress.

Other good ways of promoting suppleness are dancing,

energetic swimming and cycling. The great thing about dancing, of course, is that it takes two. Ballroom dancing is a skill men and women of sixty plus are much more likely to have acquired than even the fifty-year-olds, much less the younger generation – who don't know what they're missing. Get back out there and waltz.

Lessening strength is an inevitable part of getting older – but it does not have to be a dramatic or steep decline. The stronger you are the more likely you are to be able to maintain your independence in old age; but we don't have to look that far ahead to realise how much less satisfying life would be if you couldn't sit up in bed without a struggle or move an armchair with ease so you could vacuum underneath it. Strength can be maintained by swimming, digging the garden, using the rowing machine in a gym or weightlifting. You can buy small hand-held weights in a sports shop – or build up your arms with two bags of sugar or two cans of tomatoes when you're putting the shopping away.

Stamina means staying power – being able to continue with physical activity without getting out of breath quickly or feeling your knees turn to jelly. Maintaining stamina with exercise like energetic walking or swimming is good for the heart, lungs and circulation as well as the muscles themselves.

Do not launch into a high-powered exercise regime – start gently and work up slowly to a level that is appropriate for you, always taking a rest when you feel you need to. Check with your doctor if you have a history of heart disease, high blood pressure, diabetes or back pain before starting an exercise programme. And don't take exercise if you are feeling tired, in case you pull a muscle.

If taking exercise makes you think of doing drill or being chivvied round the school playground, think again. Think simply in terms of keeping your body active so that you can enjoy life, rather than having to hold back from it. This is not about being Superman or Wonderwoman, but being fit.

The benefits of exercise – suppleness, strength and stamina

– can also enhance your sex life. Sexual activity is, in any case, a form of exercise that can do you a power of good.

Exercise increases levels of certain natural hormones in the brain which simply make you feel good. Just taking a short walk around the park will really make you feel better – do it once, and register the positive effect of the fresh air and movement, the interest in who and what you've seen. Do it every day for a week and you'll be hooked. There is also evidence that people who take regular exercise have greater mental agility – so as well as keeping your body in good shape, exercise lifts the spirits. People who go for regular walks, or bike rides, or a swim, know at first hand what it means to 'blow the cobwebs away' and 'clear the head'. Exercise is also an aid to restful sleep.

REST WELL

There is an old country saying: 'After dinner, rest a while; after supper, walk a mile.' Modern research has proved the wisdom of these words. Body temperature and metabolism take a dip between 2pm and 3pm, so you feel sleepy. A nap taken at this time will give your energy a boost. An evening walk after your last meal of the day is good for the digestion and helps to prepare the body for rest.

That last meal should not be taken too late. If the process of digestion is just getting started at 9pm it will interfere with sleep. Quality of sleep seems to matter more than quantity as we get older. Rather than worrying because you no longer 'get your eight hours' it can be liberating to realise that you actually don't need it any more. Having said that, series of nights broken by having to get up to go to the bathroom or throwing off the covers in a sweat can leave the sufferer and his or her partner tired and tetchy. If this is the case, do what you can to deal with the underlying problem.

Men who need to pass urine frequently in the night may have a prostate problem (see p 206) and should see their GP for a check-up and advice on managing the condition. Emptying the bladder frequently during the day will help. Refraining from too much alcohol is also recommended.

The night sweats that afflict many menopausal women are the nocturnal equivalent of daytime hot flushes, and will eventually pass. Hormone replacement therapy will help to alleviate these symptoms. Women who do not wish to take HRT can help themselves to cope by wearing light cotton nightclothes and making up the bed with cotton sheets. It helps to keep a sponge or flannel and a bowl of water handy – damp skin will cool down quickly.

If you are going through a bad patch of disturbed nights and feel exhausted during the day, don't fight it. Have an afternoon nap if you can, but make yourself comfortable on a couch or in bed and have a proper rest, rather than slumping in an awkward position in front of the television.

For the great majority of people, the need for sleep diminishes in later life and we need to find ways of building our new sleep patterns into our lives while at the same time ensuring that the sleep we do get is refreshing and restful. Rather than lying awake worrying, it makes sense to get up and get on with something you've been meaning to do: writing a letter; reading a book (or starting to write one); repairing that broken plate you've been meaning to mend; listening to a teach-yourself-Spanish tape; making bread. We spend so much of our lives wishing we had more time: when we are given it, we should welcome it – even if it is 5 o'clock in the morning!

Simple, practical steps to better sleep include making sure that the mattress on your bed is supportive – get the best you can afford – and having your bedroom at a comfortable temperature, neither too hot nor too cold. A stuffy room will make it difficult to sleep well; open a window if possible. Establish a bedtime routine that you find relaxing: go for a short walk, have a warm (not hot) bath, read a book or do the crossword. Watching television until you turn the light out is not a good idea – set a half-hour 'buffer zone' between switching off the box and going to bed, using the time to wind down.

The relaxation exercises on page 239–242 can be used or modified to get you in the right frame of mind for sleep. Certain yoga exercises also have a 'stilling' effect that prepares the body for a sleep which is restorative and from which you wake refreshed.

_____ IN GOOD SPIRITS _____

A central factor in feeling good about life is relative freedom from harmful stress and being reasonably well equipped to deal with it when it comes along. In the popular imagination, stress is something that afflicts jet-setting businessmen and harassed working mothers. It isn't generally thought to be a problem for older people – as if there are no pressures in life after you have reached a certain age – or as if unperturbable serenity comes gift-wrapped on your fiftieth or maybe sixtieth birthday.

Those of us who have celebrated one or both of those birthdays know that the notion that the later years are stress-free is a myth. The issues you have to deal with in your fifties are just not the same as those that you faced in your thirties – and at seventy they will be different again. What is important is that in later life you have had years of experience that will have given you a realistic perspective on life. You have acquired the skills to enable you to deal with life's ups and downs.

A man or woman in their fifties might still be working full-time, supporting offspring through university, juggling numerous responsibilities while thinking ahead about retirement. Ten years later they may be retired, sons and daughters may be making their own way in the world, and they are learning to rediscover each other as partners. By seventy, niggling health problems might begin to make themselves felt that necessitate a slowing of pace. In the eighties, widowhood may mean increasing solitude. Just like the rest of your life, the later years present you with new situations that call for adjustment.

No life is stress-free, and too little stress in a life marked by boredom, isolation and lack of stimulation can be as harmful as too much. Problems like high blood pressure, backache and insomnia can be caused by stress. Stress can induce a sense of lethargy, depression and anxiety. Anxiety can be the trigger for drinking or eating too much, or for dependence on cigarettes. It can cause panic attacks and forgetfulness.

Any or all of these symptoms can arise in later life, perhaps when facing the demands of a new situation or coping with loss. Having the ability to cope is part of a virtuous circle. When you realise that you can deal with ups and downs and unexpected reversals of fortune, however minor, your confidence in yourself grows. You see yourself as a competent person, one who is worth taking care of and who deserves the affection of others. You give yourself what you need to be healthy; you give yourself enough time for relaxation and pleasure. You give time and energy to your relationship with your partner, and both reap the rewards. Loving yourself is not the same as being self-centred or selfish.

Being aware of your own ability to cope is an important part of dealing with stress. There are two other equally important skills: being assertive and knowing how to relax. Being assertive means being neither passive, where you always give in to other people's demands, nor aggressive, where you always get your own way by overriding the needs of others. Assertiveness is a vital skill for later life, and particularly in relationships. Without assertiveness the renegotiations that are so crucial in adjusting to a new phase become very difficult. Assertiveness allows you to say what you mean without either shrinking from it or shouting; and it allows you to listen to your partner with full attention and respect because you are not afraid of being ignored.

Lack of assertiveness bedevils many couples who don't communicate with each other effectively: where one partner believes that 'people shouldn't talk about their feelings', for example, or the other thinks 'people should know what I want'. It may feel as if being assertive carries some risks, but learning to say what you think calmly and confidently will help you to feel more in control of life and will prevent the build-up of neg-ative feelings. So, far from putting your relationship at risk, it can help to strengthen it and reinforce your love and respect for each other.

A number of books and courses offer assertiveness training for women, working on the assumption that women are more likely to be passive and need to learn how to acknowledge and express their needs. The assumption is that men are already assertive enough, but this is to fall for a double misunderstand-ing of the meaning of assertiveness. It assumes that the stereo-typical aggressive behaviour men are thought to display is assertiveness, and it is not. It also assumes that men are never passive, fearful or shy, which is simply not the case.

Men and women alike can use the skills of assertiveness to make their dealings with other people, and each other, more rewarding. Being able to state your needs or opinions clearly, to negotiate tactfully, to give and receive praise graciously makes you feel good about yourself and helps other people 'know where they are' with you. You may have to learn to speak quietly and slowly; not to rush to fill silences in a discus-sion, not to put yourself down. If necessary, prepare for a con-versation which you think might be difficult – run through some of the things you know you want to express so that you can find the words which not only say what you mean but which you feel comfortable with.

Negotiation often means compromise – if you and your part-ner have reached a sticking point over an issue such as where to have a holiday or whose relations to stay with at Christmas, being stubborn will not help. Each needs to try to understand the other person's point of view. Suppose Mary is insisting to her husband John that they spend Christmas with her family, while John wants a quiet time at home because they have been to Mary's family for the last five years. A reasonable discus-sion about it might reveal that it is Mary who needs to be assertive in order to resist the demands of her family – that she really would prefer to stay at home too, but finds it difficult to stand up for herself when her older sisters start laying down the law. The outcome might be that John helps Mary to achieve a new position of respect in the family by stating her point of view – and they both get the quiet Christmas they want.

LEARNING TO RELAX

We can find ourselves getting tense for all sorts of reasons – apprehension about a difficult situation or anxiety over a problem you haven't been able to solve. The more tense you become, the less likely it is that you can deal with the situation or solve the problem. Thoughts circle round in your head, your stomach goes into knots, your neck muscles tighten. Being able to relax your body completely is an essential first step to calming your mind.

There is a technique to relaxation which you will find useful whenever you feel tense. To prepare yourself, sit in a comfortable chair, or better still, lie down on a comfortable supportive surface. Take the phone off the hook. It is best not to have a full stomach. Empty your bladder so that you will not have to stop in the middle and go to the lavatory. Choose a quiet, warm room, when you are not too tired and where you will not be interrupted.

If you are sitting down, take off your shoes, uncross your legs and rest your arms along the arms of the chair. If you are lying down, lie on your back with your arms at your sides. Close your eyes, and be aware of your body – notice how you are breathing and at what points in your body the muscles are tense. Make sure your position is comfortable – put a small pillow under your head; you may need another in the small of your back or under your knees.

Start to breathe slowly and deeply – expanding your abdomen as you breathe in, then raising your rib cage to let more air in, until your lungs are filled right to the top. Hold your breath for a couple of seconds, then breathe out slowly, allowing your rib cage and stomach to relax. Empty your lungs completely. Do not strain. With practice, it will become much easier. Keep this slow, deep rhythmic breathing going throughout your relaxation session.

Once your breathing pattern is established, start the following sequence:

1. Curl up your toes hard and push your feet away from your body
Tense up on an IN breath
Hold your breath for 10 seconds
Let go completely on an OUT breath

2. Pull your feet towards your body and press your heels down
Tense up on an IN breath
Hold your breath for 10 seconds
Let go completely on an OUT breath

3. Tense your calf muscles
Tense up on an IN breath
Hold your breath for 10 seconds
Let go completely on an OUT breath

4. Tense your thigh muscles, straightening your knees and making your legs stiff
Tense up on an IN breath
Hold your breath for 10 seconds
Let go completely on an OUT breath

5. Tighten your buttocks
Tense up on an IN breath
Hold your breath for 10 seconds
Let go completely on an OUT breath

6. Tense your stomach, as if to protect yourself from a punch
Tense up on an IN breath
Hold your breath for 10 seconds
Let go completely on an OUT breath

7. Bend your elbows and tense the muscles of your arms
   Tense up on an IN breath
   Hold your breath for 10 seconds
   Let go completely on an OUT breath

8. Hunch your shoulders and press your head back into
   the cushion or the back of the chair
   Tense up on an IN breath
   Hold your breath for 10 seconds
   Let go completely on an OUT breath

9. Clench your jaw, frown, screw up your eyes really tight
   Tense up on an IN breath
   Hold your breath for 10 seconds
   Let go completely on an OUT breath

10. Tense ALL your muscles together
    Tense up on an IN breath
    Hold your breath for 10 seconds
    Let go completely on an OUT breath

Remember to keep breathing deeply. Be aware, as you let the groups of different tensed muscles go, of the feeling of physical well-being and the heaviness spreading through your body.

After you have completed the whole sequence from 1 to 10, and still breathing slowly and deeply, close your eyes and imagine a white rose on a blue background. Try to 'see' the rose as clearly as possible, giving it all your attention for thirty seconds. Do not hold your breath, but continue to breathe in the same rhythmic pattern you have been using throughout the exercise.

Give yourself the instruction that when you open your eyes you will be perfectly relaxed, but alert. Count to three, then open your eyes.

When you have become familiar with this technique, and want to relax at any time but only have a few minutes, do the sequence in shortened form. Miss out some muscle groups, but always work from your feet upwards. You might, for example, do steps 1, 4, 6, 8, and 10 if you did not have time to do the complete sequence.

Being fit for life means that we can be more able to love in later life, taking care of every aspect of ourselves: our physical health, the way we communicate, what we eat and drink, our sexuality, our ability to relax. Feeling comfortable and confident in ourselves can get communicated more effectively than anything else in relationships and alone can create the climate where loving, affectionate relationships can thrive. Taking good care of yourself is not about being selfish – it is an investment in the future that is your later life.

THE BEST IS YET TO BE

Here we are at the end of this book. Our intention has been to take a close look at the real lives of the growing community of older people at the end of the twentieth century.

In so many ways we are pioneers. We must embrace the opportunity to be the first generation to celebrate our right to loving in later life, however we define it – whether it is in the tenderness that comes from emotional and physical familiarity or the excitement of a new relationship that takes your breath away.

We owe it to the next generation – our children and our grandchildren – to make the difference, to be the ones who challenge ageist attitudes that limit and marginalise those who love in later life. We cannot allow ageism to stifle their hope of a future as sexual beings, confident in their right to a loving relationship however old they get.

The difference age brings to sex should not be judged by creaking bones and stiff joints but by the joy it brings and the needs it fulfils. Years and experience can bring depth and fulfilment to intimate relationships. If we can look at sexual relationships as part of a lifelong process which provides us all with continuing opportunities to grow and develop, then we can all aspire to the words of Robert Browning – 'Grow old along with me, the best is yet to be.'

RESOURCES

USEFUL ORGANISATIONS

Marriage and relationships

Relate, Herbert Gray College, Little Church Street, Rugby CV21 3AP. Tel: 01788 573241, Fax: 01788 535007, http://www.relate.org.uk
Relate offers couples counselling and/or help with sexual problems to adults experiencing relationship difficulties, whether or not they are married and regardless of age, race, personal beliefs, sexual orientation or social background. There are over 100 local centres in England, Wales and Northern Ireland. Courses are available in preparing for marriage and in starting again after divorce. Relate also offers relationship education training for schools.

London Marriage Guidance Council, 76a New Cavendish Street, London W1M 7LB. Tel: 0207 580 1087, Fax: 0207 637 4546.
This charity offers a relationship counselling service in the London area.

Marriage Care, Clitherow House, 1 Blythe Mews, Blythe Road, London W14 0NW. Tel: 0207 371 1341, Fax: 0207 371 4921, e-mail: marriagecare@btinternet.com, Helpline: (Mondays and Thursdays 3–9pm) 0345 573921.
Trained marriage counsellors offer counselling for those with marital and relationship difficulties. Local centres also provide courses for couples preparing for marriage. Marriage Care is also a resource for parents, teachers and school governors who have responsibility for the development of personal relationships and sex education.

Jewish Marriage Council, 23 Ravenhurst Avenue, London NW4 4EE. Tel: 0208 203 6311, Fax: 0208 203 8727.
Provides counselling for anyone under stress or with a problem concerning relationships, whether single, married, widowed or divorced.

Samaritans, 10 The Grove, Slough, Berks SL1 1QP. Tel: 01753 216500, 0345 909090 (24-hour national helpline or see phone book for local numbers), Fax: 01753 819004.
The Samaritans aim to help the suicidal and the despairing. There are over 200 Samaritan centres in the UK. Samaritans are ordinary people from all walks of life who choose to devote part of their spare time to helping ordinary people in distress. They are carefully selected and prepared, and work under the guidance of a volunteer director who has, when necessary, the advice of a consultant psychiatrist. Absolutely confidential service for people who are in despair and who feel suicidal.

British Association for Counselling, 1 Regent Place, Rugby, Warwickshire CV21 2PJ. Tel: 01788 550899, Fax: 01788 562189.
The BAC provides the general public with a list of counsellors in their area free of charge.

British Association for Sexual and Relationship Therapy, PO Box 13686, London SW20 9ZH. Tel: 0208 453 2707.
BASRT exists to advance the education and training of sexual, marital and relationship therapists and to promote research in the field. Send an SAE for the name of a therapist.

Help for older people

Age Concern, 1268 London Road, London SW16 4ER. Freephone: 0800 009966, Fax: 0208 6799 6069.
Age Concern works to promote the well-being of older people by helping to make later life a fulfilling and enjoyable experience.

Citizen's Advice Bureaux (CAB)
The CAB address is in your local telephone directory. It offers free, confidential and impartial advice on benefits and other money problems, rights and problems at work, illness and local organisations that can help with specific problems.

Help the Aged, St James's Walk, London EC1R 0BE. Tel: 0207 253 0253, Fax: 0207 250 4474, http://www.helptheaged.co.uk
Help the Aged provides practical support to help older people to live independent lives, particularly those who are frail, isolated or poor.

Education and leisure

Open University (OU), Postal address: Course reservations, Open University, Milton Keynes, PO Box 724 MK7 6ZS. e-mail: ces-gen@open.ac.uk, Telephone for course enquiries: 01908 653231.
The Open University is acknowledged as the world leader in part-time education and training. Over thirty years, it has successfully pioneered and developed the system of 'supported open learning' which gives people the flexibility and materials to learn from home with personal tuition via telephone, e-mail or face-to-face. More than two million people have used the OU to gain degrees or just study individual courses since the university accepted its first students in 1971.

Workers' Educational Association, Temple House, 17 Victoria Park Square, London E2 9PB. Tel: 0208 983 1515, Fax: 0208 983 4840.
The Workers' Educational Association provides adult education, independently through its districts and in co-operation with universities, local education authorities and a wide range of voluntary organisations.

Working for a Charity, The Peel Centre, Percy Circus, London WC1X 9EY. Tel: 0207 833 8220, Fax: 0207 833 1820, e-mail: enquiries@wfac.org.uk
Encourages people to consider a job in the charity world and provides a bridge to help them to take a first step towards gaining paid employment with a voluntary organisation.

Ramblers' Association, 1–5 Wandsworth Road, London SW8 2XX. Tel: 0207 339 8500, Fax: 0207 339 8501.
The Ramblers' Association promotes rambling, protects rights of way, campaigns for access to open country and defends the beauty of the countryside. Ring the number above for information about your local walking group.

REACH, Bear Wharf, 27 Bankside, London SE1 9ET. Tel: 0207 928 0452, Fax: 0207 928 0798.
Acts as a link to bring retired men and women from business or the professions (and particularly those who retire early) to work on an expenses-only basis for charities, voluntary organisations or community groups which need but cannot afford specialist skills.

University of the Third Age (U3A), Third Age Trust, 26 Harrison Street, London WC1H 8JG. Tel: 0207 837 8838, Fax: 0207 837 8845, e-mail: national.office@u3a.org.uk

U3A is a learning co-operative of older people that enables members to share any educational, creative and leisure activities. There are nearly 400 groups nationally.

Saga Holidays Ltd, Freepost, Folkestone, Kent CT20 1BR. Freephone: 0800 056 5880.
Saga offers an exciting variety of holidays for the over-fifties from UK to long-haul. There are special-interest holidays ranging from archaeology to walking and gardening breaks. Saga Holidays are only available direct and are not sold through travel agents.

Health and well-being

Al-Anon Family Groups UK, 61 Great Dover Street, London SE1 4YF. Tel: 0207 403 0888, Fax: 0207 378 9910, e-mail: alanonuk@aol.com, http://www.hexnet.co.uk/alanon/
Al-Anon offers understanding and support for families and friends of problem drinkers whether the alcoholic is still drinking or not. Alateen, a part of Al-Anon, is for young people aged twelve to twenty who have been affected by someone else's drinking – usually that of a parent. For details of meetings throughout the UK, contact the above.

Alcoholics Anonymous, PO Box 1 Stonebow House, Stonebow, York YO1 2NJ. Tel: 01904 644026, Fax: 01904 629091.
AA is a fellowship of men and women who share experience, strength and hope with each other in the hope of solving their common problem and helping others to recover from alcoholism. The primary purpose is to stay sober and to help other alcoholics to achieve sobriety. Over 3,200 groups in the UK.

Amarant Trust, 11–13 Charterhouse Buildings, London EC1M 7AN. Tel: 0207 490 1644, Fax: 0207 490 2296.
The Amarant Trust works to promote a better understanding of the menopause and hormone replacement therapy (HRT). It sets up voluntary self-help groups throughout the UK and runs menopause counselling and HRT clinics.

Breast Cancer and Mastectomy Association of Great Britain, 15–19 Britten Street, London SW3 3TZ. Helpline: 0500 245345.
This organisation offers counselling and support for women who have undergone mastectomy and information on breast prostheses.

IBS Helpline, 01543 492192 (6–8pm Monday–Friday).
The IBS Helpline offers help with problems related to irritable bowel syndrome and inflammatory bowel disease. Staffed by nurses, it is part of the Medical Advisory Service (see below).

Impotence Association, PO Box 10296, London SW17 9WH. Helpline: 0208 767 7791.
The Impotence Association has information and fact sheets about impotence. Send a large SAE for information.

Medical Advisory Service, Helpline: 0208 994 9874 (5pm–10pm Monday–Friday).
This registered charity runs a general medical helpline staffed by nurses.
Men's Health Matters, Helpline: 0208 995 4448 (6pm–10pm Monday–Friday).
This organisation deals with all enquiries relating to male health, including anything from genetic disorders, prostates, genito-urinary to cardiac. Helpline staffed by nurses.

Midlife Matters, 32 Gwynne Road, Parkstone, Poole, Dorset BH12 1ASL. Tel: 01202 735287.
A self-help group willing to help women to deal with pre-menstrual stress, hysterectomy and candida.

MIND, National Association for Mental Health, Granta House, 15–19 Broadway, London E15 4BQ. Tel: 0208 519 2122, Helpline: (9.15–4.45pm Monday–Friday) 0208 522 1728 or 0345 660163.
MIND promotes the interests and views of people suffering from mental distress in all its many and varied forms. It campaigns for good-quality local mental health services and encourages public interests and debate on all mental-health issues. Priced publications, advice leaflets and a newsletter are available.

The Pennell Initiative, Chief Executive Eva Lambert, 51 Hall Lee Fold, Lindley, Huddersfield HD3 3NX. Tel/Fax: 01484 427808.
Publications only: Free helpline 0800 550220.
Pennell is a charitable company which exists to champion, address and research the physical, mental, emotional and spiritual needs of women over the age of forty-five.

Royal National Institute for the Blind (RNIB), 224 Great Portland Street, London W1N 6AA. Helpline: 0345 669999.

The RNIB works to improve the self-determination and quality of life of visually impaired people.

Royal National Institute for Deaf People (RNID), 19–23 Featherstone Street, London EC1Y 8SL. Tel: 0207 296 8000.
The RNID works to promote equality of access to and full participation in social, economic and political structures of society for all deaf and hard of hearing people in the UK.

Women's Health Concern, National helpline: 0208 780 3007.
Provides information to women about gynaecological problems. Trained nurses supported by a panel of medical experts answer queries on all aspects of menopause, including HRT.

Support for the bereaved

Compassionate Friends, 53 North Street, Bristol BS3 1EN. Helpline: 0117 953 9639.
Compassionate Friends is a charity offering support and friendship for bereaved parents and their families by those similarly bereaved.

Cruse Bereavement Care, 126 Sheen Road, Richmond, Surrey TW9 1UR. Tel: (24-hour electronic message service) 0208 332 7227. For advice and information during office hours: 0208 940 4818.
Cruse offers counselling, support and advice for anyone suffering bereavement. There is a wide range of leaflets and publications. For a free leaflet or mail-order catalogue, please send an SAE.

Family matters

Gingerbread, 16–17 Clerkenwell Close, London EC1R 0AA. Tel: 0207 336 8183, Fax: 0207 336 8185, e-mail: office@gingerbread.org.uk, http://www.gingerbread.org.uk
Gingerbread provides day-to-day support and practical help for lone parents and their children via a national network of local self-help groups. Over 250 local groups meet regularly.

National Council for the Divorced and Separated, 168 Loxley Road, Malin Bridge, Sheffield S6 4TE. Tel: 0114 231 3585.
This organisation offers support to those who are divorced, separated and widowed. Contact them for support information and social life. There are 80 branches around the country.

National Family Mediation, 9 Tavistock Place, London WC1H 9SN. Tel: 0207 383 5993, Fax: 0207 383 5994, http://www.nfm.u-net.com
NFM's purpose is to help, through high-quality family mediation, separating and divorcing parents reach their own joint decisions, focused on the well-being of their children. NFM aims to make family mediation and supporting services available, regardless of ability to pay, to all separating and divorcing couples.

Solicitors' Family Law Association, PO Box 302, Orpington, Kent BR6 8QX. Tel: 01689 850227, Fax: 01689 855833.
The SFLA promotes a constructive and conciliatory rather than an aggressive or angry approach to resolving the problems flowing from marriage breakdown. They will supply a list of solicitors in a particular area who are members of the association and have adopted a common code of practice.

Women's aid

Northern Ireland Women's Aid, 24-hour helpline: 01232 331818.
This organisation comprises a network of autonomous local groups who provide temporary refuge for women and their children who have suffered mental or physical domestic violence. There is an open-door policy which tries to ensure that no woman is refused refuge. Priced publications are available in various languages.

Scottish Women's Aid, 12 Torphichen Street, Edinburgh EH3 8JQ. Helpline: 0131 475 2372 (Mon, Wed, Thur, Fri 10am–4pm, Tues 10–1pm).
The telephone numbers of local groups are available from your local telephone directory.

Women's Aid Federation, PO Box 391, Bristol BS99 7WS. National helpline: 0345 023468.
Provides advice, information and temporary refuge for women and their children who are threatened by mental, emotional or physical violence, harassment, or sexual abuse. There are 110 autonomous, locally based member groups offering information, advice and refuge.

BIBLIOGRAPHY

Books from Relate

The Relate Guide to Better Relationships by Sarah Litvinoff (Vermilion)
The first Relate Guide, which deals comprehensively with relationship issues from first love to retirement, concentrating on communication and using practical tasks to help couples to cope with typical relationship problems.

The Relate Guide to Sex in Loving Relationships by Sarah Litvinoff (Vermilion)
Drawing on true case histories, this book shows you how to turn a disappointing sex life into one that is enjoyable, and a satisfying one into something much better.

The Relate Guide to Starting Again by Sarah Litvinoff (Vermilion)
This guide sets out to help people to start looking forward to a positive future after the ending of a relationship. Tasks and discussion points raise awareness of patterns that are unconsciously being repeated and show how to rebuild confidence.

The Relate Guide to Staying Together by Susan Quilliam (Vermilion)
It is not unusual for partners in a relationship to reach a point of crisis. This book sets out to help them to work through the difficult times and look forward to a time of greater commitment.

Stop Arguing, Start Talking by Susan Quilliam (Vermilion)
This practical book offers a nine-point plan for couples in conflict, helping them to understand what is behind their arguments, what is preventing them from moving forward, and how to start to communicate effectively.

Sex and relationships

Crunchpoints for Couples by Julia Cole (Sheldon)
In the course of their life together every couple experiences times when the harmony of their life is disrupted. Sometimes the cumulative effect of a number of apparently insignificant problems can be a major conflict. In simple terms Relate therapist Julia Cole explains how to use these experiences to increase mutual understanding and avoid relationship breakdown.

Sex – How to Make it Better for Both of You by Dr Martin Cole and Professor Windy Dryden (Vermilion)
Whether your concerns are physical or psychological, this guide offers practical and reassuring advice.

Retirement

Retirement: A guide to benefits for people who are retiring or who have retired (Benefits Agency Leaflet RM1)
A guide to social security benefits and sources of advice.

The Which? Guide to an Active Retirement edited by Jane Vass (Penguin)
Full of ideas on planning for and making the most of all aspects of retirement.

Growing older

Time on our Side by Dorothy Rowe (HarperCollins)
Dorothy Rowe believes that our fear of growing old far outweighs the real difficulties. She shows how a rethinking of attitudes and beliefs can lead us to welcome the future.

New Passages by Gail Sheehy (HarperCollins)
The author looks at the lives of British and American people in the prime of life and explores the stages of a fulfilling adult life in the late 20th century and beyond.

Passages in Men's Lives by Gail Sheehy (Simon & Schuster)
An overview of the challenges and pleasures that begin at mid-life for men.

Physical health

Men's Health Matters by Nikki Bradford (Vermilion)
An A–Z of men's health that includes advice and information on
practically every health issue relevant to men.

Hysterectomy: What it is and how to cope successfully with it by Suzie
Hayman (Sheldon)
This reassuring book explains what a hysterectomy is, the hospital
procedure, different types of operation and their effects. Suzie
Hayman discusses the physical and emotional reactions, the attitudes
of partners, and alternatives to hysterectomy.

Coping with Prostate Problems by Rosy Reynolds (Sheldon)
A straightforward discussion of the causes of prostate problems,
the common symptoms and practical ways of dealing with the
problem.

Late-Onset Diabetes by Dr Rowan Hillson (Vermilion)
This book is essential for people with diabetes who are in their forties
or over. In detailed and straightforward language, the book covers all
the topics of interest to sufferers and shows how they can enjoy
everyday life.

The Heart Attack Recovery Plan by David Symes (Vermilion)
Recommended by the Family Heart Association, this complete self-
help rehabilitation programme explains what causes a heart attack
and how to come to terms with recovery.

How to Stop Smoking and Stay Stopped for Good by Gillian Riley
(Vermilion)
A successful and straightforward method for giving up smoking once
and for all.

Menopause

Menopause, HRT and Osteoporosis (Health Education Authority)
A booklet giving background information on the menopause, HRT
and osteoporosis which answers questions most frequently asked
by women and offers self-help tips on dealing with the physical
symptoms of the menopause, raising the issue with the family and
putting questions to your GP.

Menopause: A Woman's View by Anne Dickson and Nikki Henriques (Quartet)
The authors believe that the menopause is an important 'rite of passage' which marks a new beginning. As well as offering clear factual information and sound advice, they provide supportive encouragement for all women – and their partners – who are about to pass through this crucial phase in their lives.

Menopause by Dr. Miriam Stoppard (Dorling Kindersley)
In this illustrated guide to the menopause the author aims to enable women to be at their best through this crucial time. She considers emotional and psychological well-being as well as physiological issues and offers much practical advice.

Osteoporosis and You: Fighting the Silent Epidemic by Leonard Rose (Allen & Unwin)
A comprehensive book giving information on risk factors and associated problems, with advice on prevention of osteoporosis, treatment, and lifestyle issues including diet, health and exercise. The range of treatments available is reviewed, including HRT.

Stress and depression

Depression: The Way out of Your Prison by Dorothy Rowe (Routledge)
With sympathy and insight, Dorothy Rowe shows how, having entered the isolated state that is depression, we can make a decision to emerge from it – and draws a map of the way out.

Healing Grief by Barbara Ward (Vermilion)
A sympathetic and sensitively written guide to loss and recovery.
The Stress and Relaxation Handbook by Jane Madders (Vermilion)
A practical self-help guide in which the author, who taught stress management for over forty years, describes numerous relaxation techniques which can help everyone to counteract stress and lead a healthier life.

Be Assertive by Beverley Hare (Vermilion)
Introducing the techniques of assertiveness training, this book shows how by accepting responsibility for your own actions and expressing your thoughts in a clear and honest way, you can both communicate better and have more fulfilling relationships.

Diet

Diet and Arthritis by Dr. Gail Darlington and Linda Gamlin (Vermilion)
In this practical guide to controlling arthritis through diet the authors
give hope to sufferers.

Teach Yourself Healthy Eating by Wendy Doyle (Teach Yourself Books)
A guide to what to eat and what to avoid to stay healthy, written by a
senior nutritionist. It explains what proteins, fats and carbohydrates
are, and explodes common misconceptions about how to follow a
healthy diet. Includes chapters on contemporary eating and the link
between health and food.

INDEX